Square Wheels

Square Wheels

How Russian Democracy Got Derailed

BORIS KAGARLITSKY

Translated by Leslie A. Auerbach,
Amanda Calvert, Renfrey Clarke, and Masha Gessen

Monthly Review Press   New York

Copyright ©1994 by Monthly Review Press

Library of Congress Cataloging-in-Publication Data
Kagarlitsky, Boris, 1958-
  [Kvadratnye kolesa. English]
  Square Wheels : how Russian democracy got derailed / by
Boris Kagarlitsky ; translated by Leslie A. Auerbach.
    p. cm.
  ISBN 0-85345-891-X : $30.00. — ISBN 0-85345-892-8 (pbk.) :
$15.00
  1. Soviet Union—Politics and government—1985-1991.
2. Russia (Federation)—Politics and government—1991-
3. Moskovskii gorodskoi sovet narodnykh deputatov—History.
I. Auerbach, Leslie A. II. Title.
DK288.K35413 1994
947.085—dc20   94-11815
                                                   CIP

Monthly Review Press
122 West 27th Street
New York, NY 10001

Manufactured in the United States of America
10 9 8 7 6 5 4 3 2 1

From the Author

According to Aristotle, politics is the art of governing the city. In capitals and great cities, all of society's political dilemmas, contradictions, and conflicts are found in concentrated form. Here, theories and ideologies face a daily, if not hourly, reality check; here, the honesty of public figures is constantly being tested.

When I was elected to a deputy's seat on the Moscow City Council in the spring of 1991, I had no idea how pivotal a role the Council and the events of the next two-and-a-half years would play in my political and personal life, affording me a deeper understanding of my country, of the city in which I live, and, above all, of myself: of my role and responsibility in the events taking place around me.

This is the story of what I was able to make sense of between spring 1990, when Russia and Moscow held their first (relatively) free elections, and fall 1993, when the victorious regime of "people's president" Boris Yeltsin dismantled democratic structures like the Council. This brief period of relative freedom constituted what was for all intents and purposes Russia's sole practical experiment with democracy in seventy-odd years. It was both the zenith of Gorbachevian perestroika and its downfall.

While I hope my readers will find a modicum of entertainment in these pages, for me this book and the events it deals with represent something of a tragedy as well. For it is the story of how we failed to make use of the freedom we had acquired and let it slip from our hands.

Publisher's Note

In describing political forces in Russia, Boris Kagarlitsky broadly refers to "democrats," "communists," and "socialists." These groups are generally named informally rather than as members of specific parties. The term "democrats" refers to opponents of the old regime, supporters of economic reforms who tended to approve of Yeltsin's privatization policies. The term "communists" refers to those favoring restoration of the Soviet Union, in most cases advocating a mixed economy. The term "socialists" describes those who opposed both the pro-Yeltsin camp and the old party die-hards, and favored defense of democratic rights, workers' living standards, and public property. For a more detailed analysis of political tendencies in Russia during the period, see Alexander Buzgalin and Andrei Kolganov, *Bloody October in Moscow: Political Repression in the Name of Reform* (New York: Monthly Review Press, 1994), pp. 18–24.

"In that *direction*," the Cat said, waving its right paw round, "lives a Hatter: and in that *direction*," waving the other paw, "lives a March Hare. Visit either you like: they're both mad."

"But I don't want to go among mad people," Alice remarked.

"Oh, you can't help that," said the Cat, "we're all mad here. I'm mad. You're mad."

"How do you know I'm mad?" said Alice.

"You must be," said the Cat, "or you wouldn't have come here."

1

HOW DOES one get nominated? Will the voters turn out?

These two questions preoccupied many activists and leaders of opposition groups in fall 1989. Elections had been announced for the following spring, and this time the myriad hurdles the powers-that-be had imposed to screen out undesirable candidates during the March 1989 election of USSR People's Deputies would be gone. But the previous year's experience had taught those of us who proudly bore the mantle of the "democratic opposition" that our failures frequently revolved around our own disorganization rather than the machinations of those in power. The Moscow Popular Front, which at the time was the capital's largest and most powerful non-Communist organization, had attracted thousands to rallies during the summer 1989 Congress of People's Deputies, but when the rallies ended and people dispersed, we discovered that there were only a few hundred of us left.

People were obviously disillusioned with the results of the Congress. Everyone seemed to have lost faith in the election process. Public opinion research conducted in the capital indicated that one could count on official candidates being doomed if, and only if, the voters showed up at the polls. But there was no guarantee they'd do so.

In order to even campaign, an opposition candidate had to be running from somewhere. Neither the Popular Front nor other opposition groups had been officially registered, and so they had no legal right to nominate candidates. The only alternative was to be nominated by a labor collective. To this end, a Moscow Voters' Union (MOI) was created. Its initial function was purely technical, trying to find "nominating platforms"—places to run from, i.e., institutions and businesses where, at an organized meeting of a section, shop, or subunit, the official papers needed to nominate a candidate could be drawn up. At the same time, it was necessary to keep a constant watch so that, in cases where several democrats were running simultaneously from the same district, they didn't stand in each other's way. Despite appeals to "coordinate efforts" and "offer solidarity," candidates never-theless interfered with each others' campaigns at every step—sometimes as a result of the irresponsibility of the "freedom fighters"; at other times, for less savory reasons.

During the entire nomination period, all the "candidates for candidacy" listed in the rolls of MOI existed in a state of military preparedness. At any moment, the phone might ring with news from one of the volunteers that a "platform" was ready and you'd better rush right there. Upon arriving, you'd usually discover that the people hadn't shown up, or the necessary papers couldn't be drawn up, or something else was wrong. After three or four such instances, I was about ready to give up the whole notion, but acquaintances who'd learned of my difficulties in getting on the ballot found me a spot.

The election districts were divided more or less intelligently, although by some strange coincidence, virtually all the leaders of the Moscow socialists (the non-Communist left) encountered a minor glitch when additional democrats turned up in their districts. It's still unclear whether this was due to political hanky-panky, or whether it was just a matter of the usual muddle. In any case, at that point, there was no danger of damage to our election chances.

Political activism in Moscow had been on the rise since late January. There was no real political crisis to speak of, but opposition activists persisted in holding rallies, the authorities duly condemned these rallies, and the escalation of the usual campaign mud-slinging heated things up and piqued public interest. By February, millions of people in Moscow and all over Russia had come to feel that they'd been granted an historic opportunity to select their own new leaders and thus lay to rest the CPSU's decades-long monopoly of power.

Most of the opposition leaders hailing from the ranks of USSR People's Deputies, and a significant portion of the activists of the independent group, were, at that moment, still CPSU members, but public anticommunist sentiment was increasing rapidly, and the opposition couldn't afford not to exploit this.

On February 4, thousands turned out to demonstrate in the city, organized under the umbrella of the "forces of democracy." For the first time, all these opposition groups not only went out together onto the streets, but genuinely felt a sense of solidarity—with each other, and with the "silent majority" of people disaffected from the regime who had no knowledge whatsoever of the minutiae of democratic politics. Some 250,000 people were out on the streets, kilometer after kilometer of Muscovites standing ready to welcome the demonstrators.

The demonstration was peaceful and festive. A police officer strode in front—it looked like General Myrikov, well-known to Moscow oppositionists as a specialist in breaking up unsanctioned rallies, and now charged with protecting this sanctioned demonstration. By all accounts, it must have been Myrikov who determined the route of march. Directly behind him was an enormous banner: SEVENTY-TWO YEARS—TO NOWHERE, a very public announcement of where we had come from and where we were heading. Each group tried to attract attention to itself by displaying as many placards, banners, and slogans as possible. Representatives of the Ukrainian nationalists stood out in particular; there were perhaps two or three dozen of them in all, but practically every one came equipped with a huge yellow and blue Ukrainian flag. Scattered throughout the throng and holding their flags high, they created an impression of a thousands-strong mass. There were socialists and monarchists and anarchists; red carnations and Orthodox icons. It was a striking, colorful procession.

When illegal rallies were held in 1988 at Pushkin Square, people had hastened to avoid passing through the square. Old fears and memories of unpleasant repercussions were reawakened. One old woman, looking at the student anarchists of the "obshchina" (communards) group striding towards the square under their black banner, had moaned: "Lord, the pirates are already on the streets!" From time to time, someone had been picked up or arrested, and each demonstration was accompanied by a powerful police presence. Generals Myrikov and Postoyuk had commanded the forces of law and order with enthusiasm: standing in the middle of Pushkin Square surrounded by numerous aides, bodyguards, and adjutants, they had issued a continuous volley of orders and listened to reports. It was reminiscent of Napoleon on the field at Austerlitz: all either of the generals needed was a drum, a white horse, and a three-cornered hat.

But now all that was in the past. Muscovites were becoming accustomed to mass rallies and demonstrations. Fear was just a memory and as yet there was no bitter disillusionment, just the joy of liberation. Spring had begun. You wanted to gulp down the air and cast a loving eye on the whole world. Unfortunately, this was the one and only day on which Moscow was to experience a genuine mass democratic movement.

But there was another side to the proceedings. While some were engaged in preparing the demonstration, drawing the posters, and sewing flags, others were busy setting up the stage for a mass rally at Manezh Square. The arduous business of organizing the speakers' platform brought back memories of what had gone on at Luzhniki [the area around Moscow's Lenin stadium where rallies were held from 1989 through 1990] during the first Congress of People's Deputies. Who wasn't dying to get onto the platform in those days? Trendy intellectuals, genuine nuts, leaders of political groups with only a handful of members but with dreams (at times, not without reason) of heading a mass movement and party and occupying ministerial offices, ordinary decent people, and the usual fools, all pushed each other around, trying to grab the microphone, which was guarded by several dozen Moscow Popular Front activists. Someone was always being a pain, refusing to yield the floor or to keep to the time limit. On one or two occasions, a would-be speaker was even pushed off the platform.

This time, everything was different.

MOI was responsible for organizing the rally, with "political questions" being settled by leaders of the liberal opposition among the USSR People's Deputies. Gavriil Kharitonovich Popov opened and chaired the rally. During those hot summer days in 1989, parliamentary orators had exercised their voices in the Kremlin, and Luzhniki had been in very different hands. This time, however, the Moscow Popular Front activists, veteran leaders of rallies, were stunned to find that no place had been allotted to them on the stand. One monotonous speech followed another, in an order reflecting each orator's place in the new democratic nomenklatura. Nothing had been left to chance: the platform was fenced off from the crowd by police, who wouldn't let anyone through except by special permission.

When my turn came, and I was able to look around me on the platform, I was struck by the grim mood of a number of the speakers. Some had been given the floor too late, others had been forced to allow a rival to push in ahead of them; this would eventually mean loss of influence and the unlikelihood of being given a good position in a future democratic administration.

By all accounts, the behind-the-scenes squabble was intense, and didn't end until just before the demonstration. Yury Afanasyev's gloomy silence was especially noticeable. It was the beginning of a crisis in his political career: he'd gone up against Gavriil Popov for the right to open and chair the rally, and had lost. It took a long time to decide whether or not to allow the socialists to speak. In the end, Mikhail Milyutin and I were given permission to speak, but only as individuals. We had been too prominent at Luzhniki and before the Moscow Popular Front to deny us permission. In any case, we were relegated to the very end of the line.

Still, most of the day wasn't like that. The city had found its voice. People hadn't come to Manezh Square for political oratory; they wanted to be free. And they were free. From fear, malice, and suspicion—at least for a day.

The second pre-election demonstration on February 25 was already a different matter. Afraid of the growing spirit of opposition, the powers-that-be did everything possible to spoil the mass march. On television and on the radio, and in the official newspapers, people were urged to stay off the streets. They were intimidated with warnings of violence from extremists and police clashes. The capital looked like a town under siege. Red Square was blockaded by army and police trucks, and police paraded along the sidewalks flaunting their new helmets. Many of them carried gas masks as well.

Nevertheless, thousands of Muscovites disregarded the warnings and poured out onto the streets. The mood of the February 25 crowd was completely different from the crowd on February 4, and so was its makeup: there were fewer members of the general public, and activists from various groups had a much higher profile. And, for the first time during the era of perestroika, ultra-right-wing anticommunist groups clearly predominated.

This time, too, a battle took place behind the scenes. The rally's organizers, attempting to reach a compromise, came up with one for the books: two stands were erected, on which competitors—Gavriil Popov on one, Yury Afanasyev on the other—vied for attention. For Afanasyev, this was faint consolation for what had happened to him on February 4. He'd already lost the power struggle within the Democratic movement.

The leaders of the parliamentary opposition solemnly read out the list of "reliable" candidates they were backing for election as deputies to the Moscow City Council and the Russian Parliament. Among the endorsed was DemRossiya [Democratic Russia, a political coalition set up in Moscow by radical reformers uniting the Moscow Popular Front, the anti-Stalinist association Memorial, MOI, and various ecological groups and democratic political clubs]. At this point, the movement had neither an overall structure nor representative organs. It lacked a clear-cut, intelligible platform. In Moscow, its candidates were running on "The city for its citizens" platform prepared by socialists from the Moscow Popular Front (in fact, Oleg Ananian and I had been pretty much responsible for this entire document). During the election campaign, we'd had a chance to talk with the editors of *Argumenty i fakty* ("Arguments and Facts"), the country's largest-circulation weekly, and, after the usual waffling and delays, the newspaper had published an interview in which we laid out our program. DemRossiya adopted a similar document of a more liberal cast for Russia. No one had given any consideration to the discrepancies between these documents, or to how they were to be implemented. I suspect that few candidates had read them through with any attention anyway.

Possessing neither a coherent program nor a clear-cut political profile, DemRossiya didn't look much like a coalition poised to grasp the reins of power and govern the city or country. The group hadn't even bothered to assure the voters it would try. Neither individual candidates nor the movement as a whole had uttered a single word about the need for competent administration—that wasn't what the voters were interested in. Apart from its role as a collective voice of protest, DemRossiya had gone on to present itself to the city's unsophisticated electorate as simply a bunch of good guys confronting an evil system.

We were all aware that the existing system was lousy. Newspapers, television, and movies had been telling us for years that it was "impossible to live like this." But we still had to figure out how else to live and whether the guys marching to power under the flag of "Democratic Russia" were as good as their claim. Many of the future deputies, indeed, had no idea about the tasks that lay ahead.

The individuals and groups that the MOI apparat had put on the rolls and that the parliamentary leaders had seen fit to endorse were presented as members of DemRossiya. There was little discrimination: all who came forward were entered, regardless of their views, so long as they opposed the old regime and the lists were confirmed by the parliamentary leaders without hesitation.

If in that previous fall, when, in effect, it had only one major objective to achieve, MOI's "election machine" had kept stalling, now it quickly gathered momentum, transforming itself into a political apparat ready to make decisions and select personnel. For whom and to what ends would eventually become clear.

The 1990 elections were the first and last of their type. The infinite variety of artificial barriers to political activism were lifted, and the panoply of obstacles that confront independent candidates in even the most open of democracies hadn't yet arisen.

Moreover, it was an unbelievably inexpensive campaign. The government had kicked in 100 rubles or so for each candidate. This sum—pathetically low even for that period (half of the average monthly wage)—was used mainly to duplicate platform texts and informational leaflets. Duplication of leaflets was the biggest expense, but in many cases it was done gratis or at discount rates by sympathizers working for government institutions. The official press and television, of course, didn't give the representatives of the Democratic camp a chance to air their views, but this was just as well since people were suspicious of what was represented in this media anyway.

It would only take a few energetic volunteers to win the campaign. The City Council election districts were small enough to be traversed by foot in forty minutes or so. A few daily attacks, and all the entrances to buildings, bus stops, and shop doors could be plastered with handmade signs and xeroxed leaflets. Professionally printed signs and leaflets, as a rule, were treated with suspicion as evidence of a candidate's links to the power structure.

In general, the candidates backed by the official camp looked pretty feeble. During the registration of candidates, the head of a district electoral commission hadn't been able to refrain from asking one of them if he was running in the elections of his own free will.

The only problem that came up was the systematic ripping

down of fliers. In my district, the culprits weren't so much the supporters of other candidates as guys from Pamyat [an extremist, anti-Semitic right-wing splinter group] and other quasi-fascist groups. In fact, they were really the only people who made any serious effort to interfere with DemRossiya's chances in the elections. They tore up our fliers, scrawling six-pointed stars on them, rousing support for the nationalists running on the Fatherland ticket (a group just slightly to the left of Pamyat and which, in contrast to MNF or MOI, was officially registered and had no difficulty getting on the ballot). Our activists lost their tempers and began drawing swastikas on the Fatherland fliers.

People would often go off in twos to stick up the fliers, really just because it was more fun that way. There was no confrontation in my district. Nor was there, strangely enough, in any of the other districts. The news got to us pretty quickly that Pamyat would be passing through our district at about 10 p.m. At 10:30 p.m. our activists were out on their rounds, and by morning new fliers were back up everywhere they'd been torn down. Pamyat never returned for a second try; they had neither the time nor the people. My most assiduous assistant in all this was Daniil Borshevsky, a well-known activist in the environmentalist movement in Moscow who, luckily for me, lived in the district. Two weeks after the elections, while I was out of town, Daniil was killed when he fell under a trolley. I never had a chance to thank him for all his help in getting me elected.

As expected, the elections came out looking like a triumph for DemRossiya. Many of us were voted in on the first round, including one of the socialist leaders, Vladimir Kondratov. Kondratov chucked his original plan for the electoral campaign when families with above-average numbers of children in his district had seized an empty block of flats originally built for CPSU and KGB functionaries. Instead of concentrating on his planned campaign, Kondratov spent day after day in the building, where he used his deputy's immunity to shield the squatters from official harassment. It was time well spent; on election day, the residents of his district were 100% behind their hero, whose exploits had achieved the status of near-legend.

I wasn't the only DemRossiya candidate in my district. As a social experiment, this election provided excellent evidence that a socialist could easily beat out a liberal as soon as infighting began in the democratic camp. This was confirmed by the election of other socialists who'd also found themselves confronted by democratic rivals thanks to the ineptitude or evil designs of MOI functionaries. This gave us a heartening sense of self-confidence and independence when we eventually joined City Council. We didn't owe anyone any favors; we'd made it on our own.

There were no surprises in the second round of elections. In every instance, DemRossiya candidates who'd led in the first round made it in. For some reason, the victorious official candidates included a large number of police. Several KGB officers were also elected deputies to the Council; they got in by attaching themselves to various blocs, some favoring the party line of the CPSU Moscow gorkom [city committee of the party], uniting together in the Moscow bloc, others favoring DemRossiya or the independents. The Moscow bloc started off with about ninety members, but many later switched allegiance.

The elections ended in total catastrophe for the Fatherland group. With candidates in nearly all the districts, they only managed to get nine people elected, one of whom left the group immediately after his victory.

Following the March elections, DemRossiya had at its disposal an overwhelming majority in the City Council. It also dominated—although not quite so overwhelmingly—the Russian parliament and Lensoviet [the Leningrad Soviet]. The real problem now was to figure out just what this DemRossiya really was.

2

AT THE BEGINNING of the 1930s, my maternal grandfather, Nikolay Nikolaevich Pomerantsev, at that time one of Moscow's leading experts in antiquities and restoration, was arrested for trying to "sabotage" the reconstruction of Moscow. Pomerantsev's crime consisted of having written a letter to various government authorities, pleading with them not to raze the following historic buildings: the Sukharev Tower, the Cathedral of Christ the Redeemer, and the Mossoviet, the former residence of the Moscow Governor General. Pomerantsev was tried and sent into exile. But all the same, it was decided that one of the aforementioned buildings should be saved—rebuilt, rather than demolished. Bidding farewell to Moscow, Pomerantsev walked along Tversky Street and cast one last glance at the big red home of the Moscow Soviet. The building was in scaffolding; inside, reconstruction was proceeding apace. "For this we fought...." sighed the restorer as he set out for a ten-year term of exile in Siberia, little knowing that half a century later, his grandson's life would be so closely bound up with the red building.

Despite the Stalinist remodeling, the building has been fairly well preserved. The Mossoviet, it would appear, is the only example of a genuine late classicist building to have been reconstructed in pseudo-classicist style. Its unique combination of the elegance of an aristocratic private residence of the 1820s with the official style of the Stalinist era is striking. Part of its attraction is that even after spending months there, you can never be sure what awaits you around the corner. It was only during my second year as a deputy that I discovered, in a secluded corner of the building, a charming and very peaceful library, which more experienced colleagues—old-time apparatchiki [Communist bureaucrats]—had been using for private discussions.

Acclimating myself to this building was no easy matter. I had first set foot in it during the first 1988 Moscow rallies, when we had been trying in vain to get permission to hold a legal outdoor assembly. With Andrey Babushkin and Andrey Isayev, other leaders of the "informals" [members of any group of the counter-culture, from political activists to right-wing punks], I had gone to meet with Yury Vinogradov, then secretary of the City Council, who, of course, had refused our request, albeit politely. In the spring of 1989, Vinogradov had been the only representative of the city bureaucracy to come out onto the square and speak to the angry crowd. Demanding an end to press attacks on Yeltsin, we had been in that crowd, and we had viewed the Mossoviet as an enemy citadel that sooner or later would be stormed. Its corridors were incomprehensible labyrinths, and something dire seemed to await us in every office.

Now, after a few months, I'd become accustomed to seeing deputy Vinogradov at City Council sessions: he'd quit his job and become one of the most clearheaded and moderate leaders of the communist group. Babushkin, along with other DemRossiya candidates, had been elected a deputy, while the anarchist Isayev had only been a few votes short of being elected.

Little by little, the building became more familiar and less hostile—almost home. We began to take stock of our new position, making an effort to understand what it would mean to be responsible not only for the great red building at 13 Gorky Street, but for the entire city. No one expected the transition period to be easy. Everyone was waiting for a clash between the Council's new democratic majority, and the CPSU gorkom and its backers concentrated in the Moscow group. Although conflict eventually did arise, it turned out to be less dramatic than many deputies had anticipated.

The Moscow group hadn't organized any systematic obstruction of the Council's work. The first session featured passionate debates about procedural questions, but the Council hit its stride a lot faster than the Lensoviet. There, the democratic majority split right at the start into warring factions.

In Moscow, DemRossiya succeeded in preserving at least a semblance of unity. With 281 votes at our disposal, we could easily carry any issue as long as we managed to come to an agreement among ourselves. But in reality, from day one, we made more trouble for each other than we suffered at the hands of the communists. From day one, long lines snaked up to the microphones on the floor. There wasn't a single deputy who didn't try to grab a spot in front of the TV cameras to let his constituents see how gung-ho he was. But this display of energy inevitably led to a backlash against the delegates. Caught up in visions of mounting the podium, they were oblivious to the fact that Muscovites regarded many of them as a joke.

Even before the first session opened, the democratic majority's own meetings were marred by a ridiculous hullabaloo as deputy Lev Balashov insisted that the first order of business be the removal of the bust of Lenin from the assembly hall. A number of those present disagreed loudly; the leaders of Dem-Rossiya were especially firm in their defense of the bust. They had no particular sympathy for Lenin, but they feared—with reason—that the communist deputies might take offense and walk out if the bust were removed which would break up the quorum and interrupt the session's work. Therefore, Lenin must be left in peace for the time being.

Balashov was still determined to have his way. A few people tried to reason with him; someone yelled, someone laughed, another person tried to argue seriously.

Unfortunately, the bust of Lenin turned out to be the single most concretely debated issue at these meetings. What followed was even worse. Someone shouted that the meetings were being conducted undemocratically. Fanatic housewives, supporters of

Gdlyan and Ivanov, crashed the assembly hall, demanding that the council immediately declare a strike as a sign of solidarity with those warriors against corruption. Popov argued in favor of democracy and against totalitarianism, while offering the latest political gossip about Gorbachev and Yeltsin. Accompanying all this was the slamming of doors, shouting, and murmured gossip. It was like some demented anthill.

At first, some of the deputies seemed to regard this insanity as a triumph for democracy. Others despaired. I gazed around, wondering just how much of this crowd could, given favorable circumstances, be molded into a parliament for the city. In the back rows, I noticed a burly guy with a mustache despairingly raise his hands to his head.

"My God—" he kept saying, "—and these are democratic deputies!"

"You expected something better?" I couldn't resist asking.

"No one could have imagined this," he replied.

Within about a month, this man, Sergei Petrovich Pykhtin, would become head of the Cheryemushkin district council, and eventually one of the leaders of the inter-district opposition that would attempt to put some brakes on the arbitrary rule of the Council's new presidium. But for now, the assembly of deputies was turning into a chaotic rally. Procedural questions took up half the day, speeches dragged on endlessly, and the lines for the mikes looked like the lines for vodka.

The Council's downfall was computer games. Every time some document had to be drafted, it would turn out that a bunch of deputies were tying up the computers with simulated tank battles or car races.

By my calculation, during the first session, 80 percent of the editorial commission's computer hours were devoted to games, the remainder to its actual work. Much the same thing went on with the computers serving the standing committees. Still, it would be wrong to assume that this had a negative effect. If the computers hadn't been used for games, more likely than not they'd have been standing there idle.

The universal passion for computer games created another

problem: during the sessions, the deputies were not to be found in the assembly hall, but clustered around the computers, heedless of votes being taken. Some decisions had to be put off for lack of sufficient bodies on the floor. The computers' only competition came from the cafeteria.

The stock of games kept on accumulating. They were pirated rather than purchased, and this led to its own problem in the form of imported viruses. Programs had to be monitored continually, and the programmers were kept hard at it. Games were generally copied onto the hard disk (which we for some reason call a "Winchester") on which programs and important documents were stored. The next thing we knew, the Winchester would be out of space. This drove the programmers crazy: periodically, they'd wipe the disk clean of all game software to make room for serious programs, but soon the whole cycle would start over again.

There were lots of games, but at any given moment, one always reigned supreme. During the first session, the big hit was "Tank Warfare," where the object was to destroy the Russian hordes invading West Germany. During the break between sessions, this game lost ground to another more sophisticated game: simulated dogfights in the Near East, in which the object was to shoot down Soviet MIGs over the Persian Gulf. By the end of the second session, though, the undisputed winner was a game created by the programmers themselves, called "Perestroika."

The game's background was a swamp filled with a vast number of hummocks continually rising and falling underwater, through which the green protagonist, the Democrat, ran. Chasing the green blob, and as often as not by the end of the game swallowing it up, was a monstrous, toothy Bureaucrat. Whenever the Democrat fell into the swamp (and drowned) or was swallowed up, the same question would flash on the screen: "Shall we continue with perestroika?"

This game seemed to convey a more accurate sense of the political situation than any number of newspaper articles. Both icons were equally repulsive, and the players had no compassion to waste on the drowned or devoured Democrat. He was, at most, worth a laugh. Not that Moscow's residents were doing much laughing.

Prior to their election to the Council, several of the deputies had been regular habitues of psychiatric institutions. Not Brezhnev's infamous psikushkas [psychiatric prisons], where dissidents were incarcerated, but ordinary, therapeutic mental hospitals. I was under the impression that we had no less than a dozen of these cases among us, but I was wrong. A representative of the Council leadership confided to me that he knew of seventeen individuals—4 percent of the deputies—who were being treated for psychiatric disabilities. That was twice the percentage in the general population. Thinking back on how the elections had been conducted, it wasn't all that surprising. The main thing had been to rout the communists: everything else would take care of itself.

All the same, even the most neurotic and overwrought demonstrated a capacity to learn. People were gradually getting a grip on themselves, practicing to speak intelligibly and, most importantly, to listen to those around them. Unfortunately, though, it was impossible to carry on normal work. The atmosphere was too unsettled; even the most disciplined person couldn't help but be distracted.

Practically every day, the deputies were confronted by pickets at the entrance to the Mossoviet. Sometimes it was Pamyat condemning the "Zionist conspirators" who had infiltrated the Council; at other times it was groups of housewives and pensioners enthusiastically waving signs extolling the government's wisdom and the greatness of Yeltsin and, later on, that of Moscow's own Popov and Stankevich as well. At times the picket signs were somewhat ambiguous, for example: "Gavriil Popov, Sergei Stankevich, our life is in your hands!" On several occasions I encountered picketers who didn't have any demands but just wanted to remind us of certain issues, for instance that housing construction in the city had been slowed. Picketers also demanded the removal of deputies they felt hadn't been legitimately elected.

Some of the picket signs had no foreseeable connection to politics. For example there was one that read, "I demand that my baby be returned. Deputy Ivanov, S.B., is disregarding the court's decision and hiding my little one (one year, eleven months) from me, its lawful mother." I wasn't acquainted with Ivanov, but to raise an infant while engaged in politics could not be an easy matter.

While the deputies squabbled noisily, a different drama was being played out behind the scenes—the battle between Gavriil Kharitonovich Popov and Sergei Stankevich for the position of Council chairman. Both candidates made assiduous efforts to avoid each other. Arriving at a DemRossiya meeting, Stankevich would try to sit as far away as possible from Popov. Each had his people, but while Popov openly spoke as the Council's future leader, Stankevich was clearly ambivalent. Judging by preliminary polling of the deputies, Stankevich had a clear edge, especially since not only Democrats, but also many representatives of the Moscow group and many independents, were prepared to back him. Nevertheless, by the time the new session rolled around, Stankevich had withdrawn his candidacy.

The official story is that he withdrew so as not to split the vote of the Democratic majority. In fact, under the current alignment of forces, the Democrats were assured a victory. According to the French system of voting in two rounds, by which the Council was operating, one of the DemRossiya candidates would automatically be included in the second round. Then everyone could unanimously support the winner. But preliminary calculations indicated that in the second round, the choice would again lie between Popov and Stankevich. Stankevich could not but have been aware of this. And yet he withdrew his candidacy.

Only Stankevich could tell the whole story—if he wanted to. But even without him, the Council was aware of a part of it. By all accounts, Stankevich was under heavy pressure from his colleagues in the Inter-Regional Group of Deputies in the Union parliament. The Inter-Regional Group had preceded Dem-Rossiya; in addition, its members constituted a notably effective right-liberal political elite whose backing had been instrumental in the victories of Yeltsin, Sobchak, Popov, and other opposition leaders.

Mutual assistance among the Inter-Regional Group leaders was a form of mutual insurance; it was based less on friendship or trust than on the tradition of the mutual protection racket. Yeltsin needed Popov in order to become the ruler of Russia; Popov needed Yeltsin's backing to win in Moscow. Stankevich, who wasn't part of the old pre-perestroika elite or the upper echelons of the CPSU apparat, and didn't control any powerful interests, was needed only as an aide and could count on support only so long as he didn't interfere with the plans of the "great uncles."

Yeltsin supported Popov, having let Stankevich know that he had no chance of support from Russia's future president or leading liberal politicians if he entered into open opposition to Gavriil Kharitonovich. There was little love lost between Popov and Yeltsin, but Stankevich clearly didn't come into the picture as a possible leader for the capital. Yeltsin knew that Popov was the type who'd go after anything he really wanted, no holds barred, and that there was no point in standing in his way. The future president of Russia and the future mayor of Moscow, each rather intimidated by the other, had decided not to compete openly. Stankevich didn't scare anyone; he had no united groups behind him, no wide-ranging connections, no backers from the power elite. It was hardly surprising that Sergei agreed to forego open contention with his rival. Posts were gracefully distributed, and Stankevich contented himself with the position of deputy mayor. The elections had been reduced to a mere formality; everything had been decided behind the scenes.

Following DemRossiya's victory in the republic elections, Yeltsin and his team quickly converted the Russian Parliament—the celebrated "White House"—into their political headquarters, from which directives flew everywhere. Yeltsin might not yet have been elected president, but he'd already gathered enormous power in his hands, which he didn't hesitate to use against Gorbachev's supporters and the national leadership, or against heretics in his own camp. It wasn't long before members of DemRossiya felt this on their own hides.

At the very last moment before the elections, the situation again became strained. Although Stankevich's public stance was that of Popov's faithful colleague, in private talks with supporters, he made it clear that he wasn't overjoyed about the prospect of becoming the number-two-man behind Gavriil Kharitonovich. This sparked new tensions. A straw vote showed that if some of the democrats failed to support Popov while the communists voted unanimously for their candidate, Bryachik-hin, there would be no victor in the first round. Then, recalcitrant democrats and independents might decline to participate in the voting and mess up the second round. This would force a run-off election in which Stankevich's candidacy undoubtedly would come up again.

The Mossoviet was like a stirred-up beehive. Clumps of democrats gathered in the hallways, whispering, glancing suspiciously at colleagues passing by, then dispersing. Popov's supporters decided to establish order in their own ranks and tried to instill "party discipline" along Bolshevik lines in the democratic bloc. A majority of the DemRossiya deputies adopted a resolution requiring everyone in the coalition to back Popov; or, should they refuse, to inform the bloc's leaders beforehand, preferably in writing. There was nothing of the sort in the communist bloc.

Of course, no one was actually counting on this demand being fulfilled; clearly, it was impossible to control the delegates' conduct. As it turned out, I was the only one who felt it politic to acquiesce. As requested, I submitted written notification in advance of my refusal to vote for Popov.

The socialist group within DemRossiya was prepared to support Stankevich as the lesser evil. There was no question of our voting for Popov, who offered the city nothing but the prospect of state property being shared out among its rich and influential inhabitants.

The future Council chairman laid out his campaign program in twelve of his allotted fifteen minutes. Half of this time was

devoted to listing the city's problems—transportation, housing, pollution, inefficiency, etc., followed by a promise that,
once elected, he would put all his efforts into improving
Muscovites' standard of living. He didn't elaborate on just
how he was going to accomplish all this. On the other hand,
the second half of his speech, dedicated to the rights and
privileges of Mossoviet delegates, was fleshed out to the last
detail. We were informed that, once elected, Popov would
make sure each of us was given an expense allowance of 100
rubles a month; moreover, anyone who wished to resign from
his job and be attached full-time to the council would receive
a handsome monetary compensation.

The debates over candidates weren't particularly interesting.
Speaking on behalf of the socialist groups, I said that we weren't
prepared to back Popov until we'd gotten satisfactory answers
from him regarding the city's future, especially with regard to
relations with the CPSU gorkom, which had the largest real
estate holdings in the city.

In fact, this was the only speech made opposing Gavriil
Kharitonovich, and his supporters took note of it. On my way to
the podium, I'd been stopped in the hallway by Vasily
Shakhnovsky, who was about to take over the Council's administrative affairs. He asked me to forego speaking.

"If you want to vote against Popov, go ahead and vote to your
heart's content, but do you have to talk about it in public?"

I don't think anyone was worried about losing the socialist
votes; there were too few of us on the City Council to affect the
course of events. But we spoiled the overall picture.

Deputy Sergei Balashov livened things up somewhat by announcing that although he was going to speak against Popov's
candidacy, he would, all the same, request people to vote for him.
Such a bizarre stance was explained easily enough: Popov was
an unpleasant individual and a dubious candidate, but if that's
what it took to crush the communists, he would have to be
supported. Balashov finished off his speech to gales of laughter.
This consolidated his reputation on the Council as a comedian.
Far from being embarrassed, he did everything he could to

bolster this image. As is often the case, there was more truth in his jesting than in any lofty phrase of wisdom.

No one doubted that Popov would eventually emerge at the head of the pack. All the same, the results of the secret ballot surprised us. At least thirty-five DemRossiya deputies broke ranks and crossed out all the candidates. Bryachikhin, the ostensible Moscow candidate, quite unexpectedly received fewer than half of his supporters' votes. At least thirty-five deputies from the communist group voted for Popov, thus guaranteeing his victory in the first round.

Muscovites celebrated the Democrats' victory and hoped for the best. In fact, a bloc of communists and liberals, united in common interest, had ascended to power in the city. The interest they held in common was plain and simple: public property had to be appropriated and shared out.

The only serious conflict between Democrats and communists throughout the existence of the new Council came at the first session—and it was over property, not power. The CPSU gorkom had readily relinquished responsibility for the city's neglected economy and political life, but when it came to matters of party property, or what the gorkom leadership considered its property, the party organs were prepared to fight to the death. The *Vechernyaya Moskva* ("Evening Moscow") newspaper, originally founded by the Moscow Soviet and subsequently co-published by the gorkom and the Moscow Soviet, had reverted unexpectedly to party ownership. Its buildings, which the Moscow Soviet's former ispolkom [executive committee, short for *ispolnitelny komitet*] had handed over to the administrative department of the CPSU Moscow gorkom [party committee], became the focus of a protracted dispute. In fact, all this constituted only a small part of the party's property holdings in the capital.

The CPSU gorkom was essentially a great business empire. Gorkom functionaries controlled huge financial resources, newspapers, real estate, etc., as Donald Trump once did in New York. When the Council convened its first session, it was forced to pay rent amounting to tens of thousands of rubles for the hall in the House of Political Education, the DPP, which belonged to the CPSU—the city council itself didn't have a hall large enough to accommodate all the deputies and visitors.

The representatives of the Moscow gorkom's administrative department complained that the rental fee was too low; it didn't even cover the overhead. They had fine words about how the CPSU made no claims to monopoly over the use of the DPP and was willing to lease it to other organizations, but as matters progressed, the truth became clear: discussions were underway with an American firm about converting the House of Political Education into an entertainment complex. I wouldn't be surprised if I were greeted some day at the doorway of the DPP by Mickey Mouse and Donald Duck, with a guide announcing: "Here are our deputies, here are the performing animals, here is the Populist Party, there's the casino and game room—something for everyone!"

At the meetings of the Council commission on civic organizations, socialist deputies brought up the subject of making the building city property. But the liberal majority was categorically opposed to this: the sacred right of private property couldn't be abrogated. Later, after the Communist Party had been dissolved and its property divided up among new government units, no one felt that way. By then, even the party functionaries had found themselves new berths and were enthusiastically doing their share in dividing up the spoils. But this was all to come after August 1991. During the first days following the elections, when the rules of the game were still unclear, the leaders of DemRossiya and the Moscow communist chiefs were very careful to preserve the equilibrium, going out of their way not to jeopardize the compromise between the two factions.

The conflict regarding *Vechernyaya Moskva* and the DPP was the only predictable bone of contention. In spite of expectations, the basic clash on the Council didn't occur between the DemRossiya and Moscow blocs, but within DemRossiya itself. Myriad splinter groups and factions began to feud among themselves, although it was hard to tell them apart, since they all seemed to be saying the same thing. Independent deputies were also at odds. For the most part, the warring factions had no coherent identity or political platform. They'd suddenly pop up and just as suddenly disappear. Groups popped up with odd-sounding names that told nothing about their politics: "Commonwealth," "Initiative," and the like. It seemed basically to be a war of all against all.

3

THE OPPOSITION'S victory was a symbol of hope for millions of Muscovites, and for us deputies as well. The composition of the corpus of deputies had been changed so radically that even the Moscow communist group was composed, for the most part, of newcomers. Every one of us was making an effort to gain a sense of his or her new role, but the Council as a whole still had to demonstrate to itself as well as to its constituents that it was really in control of the city's affairs.

Our mandate as deputies gave us the right to free entry into any institution within the city's jurisdiction, including the KGB and the police. It was not surprising that the new deputies, who included quite a number of former "informals," rushed to take advantage of this novel situation, in which individuals who, only a few weeks earlier, had been picked up by the police and dragged en masse to the police station as threats to the peace and organizers of illegal rallies, were today entering these official institutions as representatives of the authorities.

A meeting of deputies from the Council's legal affairs commission with the head of the GUVD (Moscow police) had been planned in advance. But it began badly. We were stopped at the entrance and our deputies' credentials were not accepted as entry passes into the GUVD building. Yury Khramov, who'd just been named the most promising young lawyer of the year, was reluctant to yield; instead, he pulled out the text of the law on the status of People's Deputies from his pocket and, right there on the spot, began to describe the deputy's job to the duty officers, explaining the awful punishments that lay in store for them for such a blatant infringement of deputy's rights. The officers listened, looking perplexed: they'd never heard anything like it.

Meanwhile, orders arrived from the head of the GUVD, General Bogdanov, to allow us to enter the building. After a brief tour in which we were shown equipment worthy of a place in any museum of the history of technology, we were ushered in to Bogdanov. The general introduced us to his closest colleagues. The first to be presented was the head of the investigative department, Colonel Balashov, whom I recognized as an old acquaintance—as a KGB captain (he was later promoted to major) he'd interrogated me when I was under investigation in Lefortovo Prison. It would appear his progress on the career ladder there had run into obstacles, and he'd transferred to the police.

I recalled vividly how he'd explained to me that he didn't harbor any particular hostility toward anti-Soviet types such as myself; it made no difference to him whom he was interrogating. He could hardly have imagined at that moment that our roles might be reversed. Now, it was his turn to account to me.

I'll admit that this situation had caught me unawares as well. While I was agonizing over what to say on this historic occasion, a new scandal had broken out in the assembly hall. It was caused by Andrey Babushkin, who had discovered that Bogdanov's inner circle included General Myrikov, well-known to all the "informals" of Pushkin Square.

Prior to the elections, Babushkin, Stankevich, and I had all been members of the coordinating council of the Moscow Popular Front. Babushkin, in fact, had been directly responsible for organizing rallies and demonstrations. Myrikov headed the operational service of the GUVD, which was responsible for breaking up these rallies. Today, Babushkin had come to check up on Myrikov's work.

"Do you understand now, General," Babushkin shouted in his

well-trained rabble-rouser's voice, "that you were breaking the law when you ordered me arrested?"

"Nothing of the sort!" Myrikov was indignant. "You were running around with those disgraceful slogans! Have you no shame? We did everything by the books!"

They continued to squabble for about fifteen minutes, and the deputies began to chime in loudly in support of their colleague. One accusation after another was hurled at Myrikov. Then Bogdanov decided to step in and ease the conflict. He explained to us that he'd been appointed to his position by Boris Nikolaevich Yeltsin when the latter had been CPSU head in Moscow. Things were interesting under Yeltsin, he added, but it was hard to get anything done. Bogdanov began to bewail the myriad problems confronting the Moscow police, and then hastened to wind up the meeting.

So, I ended up saying nothing to Colonel Balashov. A second opportunity never arose because, soon after this, he returned to the KGB and I, at least, lost track of him. Not that I was particularly upset about it.

Myrikov was waiting for me impatiently by the door.

"Thanks," he said.

"What for?"

"For being the only one who didn't attack me today."

I began to feel a certain sympathy for Myrikov. It was true he'd done his best to break up our rallies, that he'd sent in the police to surround us. But today, it was Myrikov who'd been humiliated and had come close to being scared. It was obvious his heart was no longer in the fight against Babushkin. Babushkin's own point of view was understandable too: he was sick and tired of having to shield his head from police batons, and he had accounts to settle with Myrikov's OMON [riot police] squads, which not only dispersed our rallies, but followed us as well. (Later, Babushkin and I found ourselves cheerfully greeting a familiar face in the corridors of the Mossoviet—it was the young man who in times past had been detailed to follow us.)

Meanwhile, celebration was wildly premature. The true root of evil didn't reside in Myrikov or even in those whose orders he'd followed. Each day spent at the Mossoviet demonstrated that claims of "victory for democracy" had no basis in fact. With every passing day, it became clearer that instead of spending our time figuring out which representatives of the old regime ought to be assigned guilt, we'd be better off taking a hard look at the distribution of power throughout the city and the country, the way the overall system operated. And the more we learned about the actual mechanisms of power, the more there was to worry about.

People not embroiled in politics were fond of saying that democrats of all stripes absolutely had to act as a united force. Politicians themselves made "unity" their daily litany. Even Western journalists, apparently forgetting the history of their own countries, gave vocal support to the idea of democratic unity.

As matters stood, such "unity" would have been a blatant sham. Most democratic politicians were concentrating on shoving their rivals away from the feeding trough. Even putting aside the personal and political unscrupulousness of individual "warriors against communism," it didn't take an advanced degree in history to figure out that democracy isn't a matter of imposed "unity" of everything and everyone, but of competition among a variety of opposing interests. A lack of delineation among interests, the inability of social forces to engage in political demarcation, nurtures dictatorship. Universal rebellion against the old gods scarcely constitutes the triumph of freedom. A change of master rarely brings happiness to a slave; most often, the new master turns out to be even worse than the old one: starving wolves are more dangerous than the well-fed.

Even at the moment of its greatest triumph, the democratic movement coalesced only as a throng at an outdoor rally. Organizational and political fundamentals were sadly lacking; people weren't sure what they were doing, what they were fighting for. Everyone expressed faith in a lovely, abstract democracy which, apparently, according to what their leaders said, existed in the West (although they had no direct evidence of this). But no one was quite certain how democratic institutions were supposed to function, why they were so important, or what they were supposed to achieve for society. When the question of what the individual deputy, or people of his social rank, hoped to get from democracy was raised—not in front of crowds of demonstrators, but before scores or hundreds of activists vying for places in the new councils—the only answer many of them could come up with was the tried and true: perks, big bucks, trips abroad, status. Weren't those payoffs available under the old regime?

The pursuit of "unity" without organization or a platform constituted an ideal breeding ground for backstage intrigues. Most questions were decided by a tight little band of leaders who had no sense of obligation to the deputies. The deputies were in a similar position vis-a-vis their constituents. The presidium looked down on the deputies, and the chairman looked down on the presidium. The cleverest and most unscrupulous of the old-line bureaucrats, having quickly sized up the situation, cast all caution to the winds. The more honest and professional ones began to tender their resignations.

After Gavriil Popov, not yet elected Council chairman, made a public announcement that he'd have bureaucrats guilty of "sabotage" sent out of town, the apparat was panic-stricken. They were all keenly aware that any shortfall, due more often than not to the incompetence of the new leaders themselves, might be construed as sabotage. One after another, they laid their letters of resignation on the table. Popov's threat was never implemented; nevertheless, it accomplished its task. Some bureaucrats left, others hastened to find themselves friends and protectors among the city's new leadership.

Under such circumstances, the real test of power often lay in turning it down: not giving up working for the city, but refusing offers of a job, a salary, a place on the presidium as most of us socialists did. Not everyone had it in them to do this.

In September 1989, meeting in London with the editors of *New Left Review*, I prophesied that after the spring elections the Moscow Popular Front might find itself at the helm of the city government.

That is precisely what happened. Meeting in the hallways of the Mossoviet, members of the former MPF Coordinating Committee would joke that, since they had a quorum, they might as well go right ahead and hold a session. The leaders of the MPF occupied prestigious posts. Sergei Stankevich had become deputy chairman of the Council; Mikhail Shneider, an aide to the chairman. Vladimir Boxer was now one of the key behind-the-scenes figures managing the Democratic bloc's day-to-day affairs, while Oleg Orlov headed the commission on freedom of the press, assembly, and civic organizations.

It's easy to imagine how surprised many in the victors' camp were to learn that neither Vladimir Kondratov nor I aspired to any posts that might have been nominally due to us in view of our "rank" as representatives of the MPF's nomenklatura. The same held true for other left deputies. *Moskovsky Komsomolets* reporter Aleksandr Popov, who'd taken over the responsibilities of deputy chairman of the commission on freedom of the press, declined the salary: experience indicated there was to be a price attached.

The presence of many MPF activists in important positions on the Council was evidence of their services to democracy, but what of the ideas proclaimed by the MPF? Were these valued as highly? All the plans to bring enterprises vital to urban life and development under city control, discussions about restructuring the city's economy, talks of extensive self-government and citizens' participation in decision-making, were forgotten instantly, buried in the written platform of the socialist party, where some of the idealistic-minded MPF activists had taken refuge.

The ideas were good for stirring things up, but the Council didn't run on ideas. At the outset of the first session, signs of sharp conflict between supporters of Popov and Stankevich began to appear. The distribution of roles in the Council presidium which guaranteed Stankevich second place did nothing to calm things down, since the rest of the presidium and the leadership of the commissions still had to be formed.

The backstage intrigues that accompanied the assembling of

the presidium weren't all that different from everyday bureaucratic battles. Each group tried to pick up its quota. The more hopefuls there were, the larger the presidium grew, and the faster the number of posts in the commissions rose. The leaders understood perfectly well that the loyalty of a deputy passed over in the distribution of posts could not be counted on, and they tried insofar as was possible not to offend anyone. Only after the two sides had divided up all the posts, did their mutual suspicion vanish, and reconciliation between the two clans begin.

The central issue of the first session following the election of the presidium chairman was election of the leader of the ispolkom. The coexistence of these two posts within a single governmental body was apparently a legacy of Gorbachev's political maneuvering. In the early days of perestroika, the CPSU General Secretary devised what he thought was a marvelous way of reconciling free elections within a single party system. Prior to his reform, the system had been relatively logical. There was a Council; it had an executive body (the ispolkom) whose leader was a mayor of sorts. True, he had virtually no authority; real decision-making responsibility lay with the Party's gorkom, which left only the mechanical details to the ispolkom. Unwilling to sacrifice party interests, but at the same time eager to strengthen the role of the Councils, Gorbachev came up with the idea, as a supplement to the ispolkom, of the position of Council chairman, this position to be occupied by the first secretary of the CPSU gorkom. Thus, the head of the Party organization would become the city's official number one, not just its de facto leader.

This reform was never implemented. The only chairman of any council of note to hold both posts was Gorbachev himself, when, in 1989, he was elected chairman of the USSR Supreme Soviet. By the time elections to the city councils came around, Gorbachev's cunning innovation had long been forgotten, although every Council now had its chairman.

Technical questions were to be decided by the leader of the ispolkom as they had been before. The Council chairman had to find a candidate for this post. At first, Popov didn't exclude the possibility of retaining the ispolkom in its previous form, but then his eye fell on Yury Luzhkov, who in the old bureaucratic system had been the city's second in command. Prior to the elections, Luzhkov had worked as deputy to Saykin, Moscow's last communist leader. Before that, he'd been in charge of the city's agribusiness complex. It's understandable that a man who'd held these posts in a society where the words "bureaucracy" and "trade" had become virtually synonymous with "corruption" couldn't help but arouse suspicion.

Accusations of corruption on Yury Luzhkov's part came up more than once, and not only in the corridors of the Mossoviet. The mass-circulation newspapers *Ekonomika i Zhizn* ("Economics and Life") and *Moskovsky Komsomolets* ran articles citing clear instances of Luzhkov's abuse of his power as head of the ispolkom (under Saykin). The articles' authors asked the deputies to investigate. But no response was forthcoming from either Luzhkov or the majority of the deputies. Apparently, except for a small group of socialists, no one took an interest in such questions. If an analogous publication—the *New York Times*, let's say—had raised doubts about the reputation of a high-ranking city official in its pages, it would have set off a scandal of massive proportions. Those suspected of shoddy practices would have either demanded their day in court to clear their name or resigned. In Moscow, contrary to the journalists' expectations, nothing of the sort could or would happen.

For too many people, regardless of where they stood in the power structure, corruption had long since become a way of life. Neither old-time communist apparatchiki nor the new democratic activists were interested in fanning the flames of such scandals. The question of morality politics had become uncomfortable for both sides. When the greens or we socialists tried to bring up this topic, we were simply ignored.

Rumors circulated in the Mossoviet of eleven volumes of materials on Luzhkov in the possession of the Moscow police chief, General Bogdanov. Even the names of the investigators who'd handled these cases were going around, but Bogdanov held his tongue, and the investigators decided not to air what they knew, especially since many accusations apparently couldn't be proved conclusively.

Luzhkov was elected without any opposition. The presidium finally got down to work. You have to give credit to the commission's leaders and the other new city officials for showing up regularly at all the meetings. Especially since, aside from dwelling on boring details of city management, discussions at these meetings focused on a slew of more interesting topics: how various street names should be changed, for example, or how to ensure that any deputy who so desired would be able to purchase a car at the government price without any wait.

The renaming of streets went on, picking up momentum like an avalanche. Each change brought another one in its wake. First, Gorky Street reverted to its original name, Tversky; and the Mossoviet itself changed its address from 13 Gorky Street to 13 Tversky Street without moving an inch. Obviously, the Gorky subway stop would have to change its name, too; in fact, reverting to Tversky meant that the name of a whole subway line—Gorky-Zamoskvoretskiy—would have to go, since there'd no longer be any Gorky station.

The subway people were pretty offhand about the new names. The same station would appear under different names on different maps; anyone unfamiliar with the Moscow subway ran the risk of getting totally lost. A visitor trying to get to the Kitai-gorod station would end up in Nogin Square, with no way of knowing that it was the same place. Even Muscovites had trouble figuring out the endless and constantly accelerating speed in name changes. The signs simply couldn't keep up with the changes.

Everything associated with the revolution and the succeeding seventy years of Soviet rule was being changed. At times, in the heat of the moment, prerevolutionary names also got changed: thus Lenino was changed, even though the area was named not for the leader of the Bolshevik revolution, but for Lena, the landowner who, a century earlier, had owned the property. Stankevich Street, on which, by an odd coincidence, the back entrances to the Mossoviet building were, kept its old name—apparently, no one wanted to offend the deputy chairman of the Council (during his time in the Popular Front also, Stankevich had confessed to being a distant relative of the revolutionary for whom the street was named.)

The question of automobiles for the deputies naturally aroused even greater interest than the renaming of streets. The budget-financial commission headed by Feinschmidt, having researched the question thoroughly, concluded that fulfilling the requirements of the community of People's Deputies would entail the purchase of five hundred automobiles which would then be sold at government prices to the deputies. Somehow, no one had realized that these cars would, of course, have to be removed from normal sales channels—and thus become unavailable to people who'd spent years on waiting lists. Only two of the presidium's members felt that this wasn't entirely ethical and voted against it. One of them was Council deputy chairman Nikolay Nikolaevich Gonchar.

4

THE LESS EFFICIENT the Council became, the more authority was concentrated in the presidium. Thus, the presidium's members weren't particularly motivated to make the Council sessions more productive. Muscovites who had the stamina to watch through the second half of the first session would be able to recall the shameful moment when the Council had to disperse because it hadn't even managed to convene a quorum to close its session!

One can criticize the deputies for this, but it wasn't simply a matter of the "low energy" which all of a sudden became a pet theme of the Moscow newspapers. The Council was simply too big to be an effective working body: with 480 deputies, not organized along party lines, it was more like a crowd at a small rally than an organ of city government. Emotions tore through the hall, swaying the crowd one way and another—that is, when a crowd could be assembled in the first place.

The ease with which the deputies could be manipulated was evident from the events of spring 1990. It all began when, under pressure from Gorbachev and liberal reformers, the USSR's doggedly conservative prime minister, Nikolay Ryzhkov, decided to put before the public his plan for the forthcoming transition to a market economy. Instead of the expected enthusiasm, the prime minister's speech incited panic. Liberal publicists hadn't yet succeeded in winning sufficient public sentiment, and only one aspect of the prime minister's speech came through: a free market meant that everything would cost more. And so thousands of people rushed into the stores and whipped everything that was left there off the shelves.

On the second day of this disaster, I ran into Gonchar in the assembly hall. He'd just returned from the Bauman district, where he'd maintained his position as district council chairman. He looked like someone who'd just returned from a battlefield where the enemy was breaking through the front lines. "Well, how is it there?" the deputies asked.

"Yesterday, all the pasta for the next two weeks was bought up. Only salt and pepper were left in the stores."

"And what now?"

"Today they came back. They're buying the salt and pepper."

As one might have expected, the Council responded to the consumer madness with a political madness of its own. The deputies acted emotionally, lacking as they did reliable information or expert advice. The ispolkom demanded that the sale of goods to out-of-towners be limited and shoppers' passports be checked to keep people from other regions from emptying the shelves of the city's stores. By the next day, Moscow was immersed in a trade war with all the surrounding regions, since the capital had long been allotted an extra quota of foodstuffs to cater to the inhabitants of neighboring districts who would come into town to buy groceries which were not available locally. The Council's ispolkom published a long list of goods whose sale was restricted to so many items per person, including men's underwear. In army units around the country, Muscovites came under attack: one man was beaten to death, and many had arms and legs broken.

Who was running the capital? The deputies had no real authority. The Party gorkom kept itself aloof, not without amusement following the Council's difficulties. Real power was divided between the ispolkom and the Council presidium. The presidium in turn comprised a number of commissions charged with drafting new laws and regulations. But were these structures capable of carrying out a common policy?

The main problems the commissions immediately came up against were lack of concerted action and our personal incompetence as deputies. It's hard to say who was more to blame—the deputies, or the voters who'd chosen these people to represent their interests. The main problem was actually structural. Under the old regime, the city's party leaders had known at the outset whom they needed on the Council commissions. If a matter required architects, economists, lawyers, whatever, they'd be hand-picked in advance. Perhaps they weren't always inspired choices but for better or for worse, the system worked.

With the advent of relatively free elections, the voters, of course, had no interest in these administrative details. What did they care who was running in a neighboring district and how many architects or lawyers would end up on the Council? The People's Deputies included a healthy number of policemen; practically no women; more teachers than doctors; lots of journalists; and virtually no specialists on urban economics. The same held true for the district councils, and the effect there was even more deleterious. At the Mossoviet, there was at least safety in numbers: out of five hundred deputies, the probability was that there'd be one or two specialists in just about any field.

I wondered how it was done in the West and was quite surprised to find the answer was: just as we did under the old system, but on a multiparty basis. Every serious party with a claim to a role in the power structure knows what specialists it needs on its team. The first order of business is to get the ablest candidates on the slate in the safest districts and thereby guarantee that they'll be elected. If worst came to worst, experts could always be added to the deputies' fractions. Commissions are drawn up in the same way, but with the participation of elected deputies from different parties. The party or coalition commanding an electoral majority controls the commissions and uses them to pursue a united and consistent policy which has been laid out in advance. Competence is combined with concerted policy actions.

Soviet citizens had celebrated the advent of a multiparty system as a necessary basis for democracy; but no one had informed the new political parties that they had to do more than simply exist. There was plenty of work for them to do, but they were paralyzed. A broadly-based bloc like DemRossiya—an assemblage of informal groups, leading independents, and political figures of various stripes—wasn't cut out for the tasks at hand. It had no unifying political program, no overall organization, no clear-cut ideological basis beyond general paeans to democracy and condemnation of totalitarianism. All this was fine for an opposition, but it was woefully inadequate for a ruling body. Some politicians, of course, like Gavriil Popov, had their own notion of how reform ought to be carried out; but for the time being they were unwilling to divulge it and therefore were unable to use it to unite their supporters.

It comes then as no great surprise that the deputies, shelving more important business, argued until they were hoarse about what to do with the bust of Lenin. Here, at least, was an issue with which they were competent to deal.

Having failed to gain DemRossiya's support in his battle against the bust which still adorned the assembly hall, Lev Balashov decided to take matters into his own hands. His impassioned speech set off a furious and protracted debate which was followed, not without amusement, by tens of thousands of TV viewers.

The battle over the bust of Lenin remains for many Muscovites the sole bright point of the Council's first session. Having failed again to achieve a majority, Balashov and like-minded colleagues hurled themselves into action and got the bust off the wall between meetings. It was no great feat of strength: the bust may have been big, but it was hollow inside. What is more, artisans had thoughtfully put it on wheels so that it could be wheeled on or off stage expeditiously, as circumstances dictated.

As usual, one bold move set off a string of others. One group of deputies wheeled Lenin out; another wheeled him back in. In order to regain some semblance of control and to avert any further shifting around of the bust, the Council leadership had to come to a swift decision. It arrived at a perfect Solomonic solution: the bust would stay where it was, but with its back turned to the hall. And there it remained, face to the wall, the deputies gazing at its back.

Was Lenin turning his back on the deputies, or vice versa? It depended on your point of view.

The whole saga was aired on TV and printed in the papers, with Balashov and his colleagues offering journalists lengthy explanations for their actions in removing (or retrieving) Lenin's bust.

In this case, at least, the city's leaders were not at fault. They'd done all they could to salvage the Council's reputation. Unfortunately, not all their decisions were so wise.

If anything got done at all, it was mainly thanks to the old bureaucracy. We continued, as before, to criticize it. But without it, the Council would have been lost. Like it or not, the old bureaucracy did exhibit a modicum of professionalism. Instead of streamlining, however, the bureaucracy began to grow, its structure becoming ever more complex. We had several bureaucracies: the presidium and the commissions had their own offices, as did the ispolkom. While the Council's 1990 budget of approximately five million rubles (not including the ispolkom budget or sums allocated for general urban expenses) seemed reasonable, when one considers how little we actually accomplished over the year, the amount was staggeringly generous.

All issues of significance were decided by the commission/presidium/ispolkom triumvirate. Here, the opportunities for power games were virtually unlimited. The Council sessions were losing any substance they might have had, especially as it became increasingly difficult to even muster a quorum.

The deputies, for their part, were confronted with the choice of concentrating either on politics in the commissions or on the affairs of their own constituencies. In a system of functioning political parties, tasks can be delegated. Political blocs routinely assign administrative and other chores according to a mutually agreed-upon division of labor (as the socialists on the Council had attempted to do). But an independent deputy was obliged to take care of everything himself, to take personal responsibility for each and every decision, to be at once politician and expediter or (in our newly adopted lingo) lobbyist. Both were needed, but it was proving more and more impossible to combine these functions. And so, political and administrative dealings were to become the purview of two very different groups of deputies.

Everywhere it was the person in the position, rather than the position itself, that counted, and relations between the local leaders big and small, rather than local interests, influenced decisions. We were witnessing a rapid deterioration toward a classic feudal system of government. Foreign experts in medieval history could have used Moscow as a living example of feudalism in action.

Almost every "ruler," like a medieval overlord, hurried to concentrate and centralize power around himself. Moscow treated the Russian government the way Russian leaders treated the Union government, while the local authorities got their own back on Moscow by declaring Moscow City decrees to be void in their areas. The concept of sovereignty without independence that served as the basic governing principle of the patchwork medieval empires became generally recognized. As in times past every overlord had felt obliged to coin his own personal currency, so now they all strove to introduce their own coupons, vouchers, and identity cards. While Yeltsin wanted a Russian currency, Popov insisted that Moscow have its own money. Since introducing separate currencies proved impossible for many reasons, the idea arose first of coupons and then of vouchers. This seemed absurd, all the more so coming from a politician who claimed to be in favor of the development of a free market. But like any overlord, the ruler of Moscow needed Moscow money to bolster his authority.

The city's problems were exacerbated by the mass of refugees who arrived in the capital from all parts of the disintegrating Soviet Union. Among the Muscovites these people aroused mixed feelings of pity and fear, particularly since the situation in Moscow itself continued to deteriorate by the hour, let alone the day. But one has to give the inhabitants of the city their due.

There were virtually no conflicts between the people of Moscow and the refugees; most Muscovites were reasonably sympathetic to them. The same could not be said, however, of the city's leaders.

When Popov was questioned on TV about the refugees, he hedged. There were, after all, he said, only a few thousand refugees in the capital, and besides, over a dozen deputies were looking into their problems. There were thousands of dogs in Moscow, he added. Why wasn't anyone worrying about them? When Andrey Babushkin, the Council deputy with responsibility for the refugees, together with the minority ethnic communities, demanded an apology, they were informed by Popov's staff that no apologies would be forthcoming since the Council chairman had said nothing offensive. According to one of Popov's aides, Mikhail Shneider (a former member of the Moscow Popular Front leadership), Gavriil Kharitonovich sincerely loved dogs and was very concerned about their welfare. At least one category of the city's inhabitants aroused Popov's sympathy.

Nothing was getting done, although a flood of resolutions poured forth from the Council. A resolution was passed to the effect that Russia's laws would take precedence over Union laws within Moscow's city limits. At the same time, the Council issued numerous city rules and regulations. The city's local authorities were snowed under with documents issued by the Council presidium and ispolkom which the latter two bodies hadn't even bothered to submit to the deputies for a vote. Sometimes the Council instructions were carried out, sometimes not. In conditions of legal chaos, anyone in a position of power, however small, was virtually free to use it as he pleased. Some Moscow districts opted to stick with the national legal system, others with the Russian. Some chose to follow City Council instructions, others simply tossed them into the wastebasket.

By now the feudal system had spread throughout the country. When the City Council restricted the purchase of consumer goods to those whose legal residence was Moscow, the rulers of neighboring regions, considering this an encroachment on their rights, retaliated in kind. Moscow was, in effect, blockaded: all shipments of goods to the capital from the surrounding regions were stopped. Sometimes even shipments in transit were not allowed through. The Kalinin region (soon to reacquire its old name, Tversky) took an especially tough stance. Back in the fourteenth century, the princes of Tver had been the main rivals of Moscow. But Tver was conquered and became a provincial town of secondary importance. Now, it seemed, the time had come for revenge. Popov was forced to make concessions. The ruler of Moscow went to Tver to sue for peace, acceding to all the conditions dictated by the victorious provincials. Some of the shipments of foodstuffs earmarked for the capital were now redirected to the neighboring regions.

Even before the trade wars, there had been a plan to rename Gorky Street Tversky. Although there was no direct connection between the renaming of the street and the conflict, the change of name was speeded up in order to appease the Tverites. In an impressive ceremony in Tver's main square, Popov informed a cheering crowd that Gorky Street would hereafter be known as Tversky Street. The victors were appeased.

5

THE MAY 1, 1990 demonstration was the first official holiday to be celebrated following the victory of the democratic bloc in Moscow and Russia. The day's traditional ritual was for a thousands-strong column of demonstrators, carrying red banners and patriotic slogans, to file past the country's leaders, who watched the scene from a viewing stand over the mausoleum inside which, guarded by armed soldiers, the mummified Lenin lay (and where, for several years, Stalin had reposed as well). Year after year, the ceremony had been repeated without the slightest alteration. The plan was to repeat it this time, too, without major changes. Times however, had changed, and there were now new public figures to accommodate.

It was somewhat disconcerting to see Popov standing on the tribune at the Lenin mausoleum along with the Communist Party leaders. He joined them in greeting the demonstrators—who might be forgiven some puzzlement as to what this self-proclaimed champion of ideological liberalism was doing in such company.

But this wasn't the day's only surprise. The traditional ritual was rudely interrupted by a crowd of anticommunists who marched into the square after the columns of official demonstrators and, stopping in front of the mausoleum, began to heckle the government leaders.

"Throw the bums out!" they shouted. Russian history had

never seen anything like it. The country's leaders, after all, hadn't ascended the mausoleum in order to have insults hurled in their faces. According to tradition, everything should have been the other way around! Gorbachev and the other embarrassed leaders left the viewing stand to the crowd's mocking cheers. Imagine the crowd's surprise when Gavriil Kharitonovich followed suit!

Homeless petitioners set up a shantytown in front of the Hotel Rossiya. Little by little, their settlement took on a life of its own, the prototype of the slums which eventually would appear everywhere. Plywood shacks gradually replaced the tents.

Such encampments of the poor, usually found in southern countries, are ill-suited to our climate. That our own town of shame managed to keep going, developing its own urban rhythms, was proof that, even in this climate, our people can survive such circumstances.

Liberal newspapers enthusiastically ran photographs of the shantytown and wrote sympathetically of its dwellers' plight—these were "victims of communism." Oddly enough, the same papers, literally the same day, published articles about the comfort of life in America, where there was apparently no poverty; if one did come across a few homeless folk there, they were either "coloreds" or just crazies whom an overly democratic legal system was reluctant to lock up in mental institutions. Among the inhabitants of Moscow's shantytown there were also, of course, quite a few people with psychiatric problems. But they, at least, were white, and therefore aroused the sympathy (if tinged with squeamishness) of the progressive intelligentsia.

Having survived the summer months without great difficulty, the shantytown's residents could certainly have made it through the winter had Stankevich not celebrated the new year by sending in the bulldozers and OMON squads who, in a single night, razed the town. Thus the experiment demonstrated not only our people's tenacity, but also the authorities' ability to get the better of them. Some deputies called for a protest, but by the time they got organized, the bulk of deputies had already latched on to some new scandal.

So it went on, one scandal succeeding another with regularity. After several months of work, the deputies had become somewhat more professional, although the passions still ran high. Balashov, who was forever leveling accusations both founded and unfounded against the city government, was twice involved in hand-to-hand scuffling. The first time, he clashed with Sokolov. Balashov attempted to grab some papers lying on a Council functionary's table. The owner of the documents protested, and Solokov, who happened to be standing nearby, calmly pinned Balashov's arms behind his back and dragged him out of the room. So began Solokov's career in maintaining law and order in the city. In fall 1991, having won the mayor's trust by his zealous service to the new city leadership, he was awarded the position of deputy chief of the Moscow KGB.

The second fight was several weeks later when Balashov hogged an assembly hall microphone a bit too long. Deputy Glushets, who was next in line to speak, tried to shove Balashov away from the mike. The latter resisted and a fight ensued.

Pleading deputy's immunity, Balashov claimed it was illegal to set hands on him. Glushets and Sokolov also enjoyed immunity, which gave them the right to hit Balashov or, at any rate, made it impossible to punish them for having done so. The investigation got bogged down and everyone decided the incident would best be forgotten. Except, that is, plaintiff Balashov.

In fall 1990, yet another scandal erupted which shook Moscow housewives to the core: City Council registered the newspaper *Tema*. This paper was published by the Association of Sexual Minorities which, according to the press, included not only gay men and lesbians, but also zoophiles, pedophiles, and necrophiles. These latter groups didn't evoke much sympathy. Passions were intensified when the Association's representative, Roman Kalinin, upon being asked whether he had encountered any difficulty in registering his paper, replied that there had been no problem since "we have plenty of supporters at the Mossoviet."

The scandal continued for several months, fanning interest in the newspaper and bringing in a steady revenue to its publishers. Roman Kalinin became a celebrity in the media, especially after he remarked in an interview, "I don't want to sleep with Gorbachev." Alas, no one asked the president himself how he felt about the idea. In the summer of 1991, Kalinin announced he was running for president of Russia. He couldn't be registered, however, as he didn't collect the required 100,000 signatures.

The establishment of freedom of the press in Moscow, in fact, deserves a paragraph or two. One has to admit that the Commission on the Mass Media and Social Organizations had adopted a very democratic stance, permitting the rapid registration of publications of almost every stripe. No steps were taken, however, to ensure any degree of regulation or control over the trade. Since the State Press Agency, possessing a total monopoly over the distribution of the official press, had gone over to "market conditions," in other words had simply raised sharply the prices for its middleman services, all the trade in the new press was pushed out onto the street. In pedestrian underpasses and all around the metro stations suspicious-looking types suddenly appeared offering samizdats.

Trade in the samizdat press had arisen in Moscow as early as 1988 or 1989. The first publications were the Democratic Union's *Svobodnoe Slovo* ("Free Word") and *Express-Khronika* ("Express-Chronicle"). Even before the Moscow City Council had passed the law about the press, the independent press had produced dozens of titles in Moscow alone. Most of the printing was done in the Baltic, although by 1989 or 1990, it became easy to find printing presses in Moscow as well.

Since, on the one hand, the distribution of such publications was fairly risky at first (one could be detained for several days, and there were cases of vendors being beaten up), and, on the other hand such business brought in enormous profits from the very beginning, a mafia-type structure similar to those which ran the drug and prostitution business came into being very rapidly. Racketeers appeared who collected protection money from the free press vendors, and various gangs divided up spheres of influence among themselves.

The legalization of such activity, without first taking steps to make financial control over it easier, allowed mafia groups to start to operate in the open and with great insolence. Beating up competitors became the norm, and walking through Pushkin Square or other centers of the trade could be dangerous.

At times, the goings-on at "Pushka," or Pushkin Square, which had become a hothouse of public debates, rackets, and prostitution, took on a comic air. When Yaroslav Leontiev, an activist of the left-radical Socialist-Populist group, showed up to sell *Revolutionary Russia*, he was immediately approached by an athletic-looking type who demanded ten kopeks for every copy of the paper sold, "to avoid any unpleasantness." When Leontiev refused, within half an hour, three other such types appeared, asking for payoffs twice as high. The crowd turned a blind eye. However, breaking the spirit of the idealistic revolutionary turned out not to be so easy.

"Citizens, comrades!" Leontiev yelled. "Look what the KGB is doing to distributors of a free press!" The crowd, who had expressed utter indifference to the racketeers' dirty dealings, suddenly turned on the "KGB agents." The three young guys, their self-confidence wilting, attempted to defend themselves. But remarks like "I'm not an agent, I'm just a thug," convinced no one. The racketeers beat a hasty retreat.

From time to time, Aleksandr Popov and Vladimir Kondratov also carried out raids on Pushka to catch speculators selling newspapers (violating City Council regulations) at inflated prices. They'd frighten off the vendors by threatening to call in the cops. The police didn't like patrolling the pedestrian underpasses and went reluctantly when the deputies insisted. At such moments, the underpasses would empty. But that didn't last for long.

Over the course of many years, Pushkin Square had been a kind of barometer of social life. In the 1970s, school graduates gathered here after their graduation parties. Dissidents too, from time to time, assembled in the square for small meetings, after which they were arrested. The biggest day for arrests was on December 10, International Human Rights Day, which dissidents marked with protests. On this day, every year, hundreds of plainclothes and uniformed police officers cordoned off the square, trying to prevent a few dozen people of like mind from gathering.

Then, Gorbachev's perestroika took off, and Pushka changed character. It seethed with rallies. OMON and members of the local police station dragged off Democratic Union (and sometimes Moscow Popular Front) activists, bundling them into buses. There were even Pushkin Square jokes. Cop to bystander: "Were you at the rally?" "No." "Quick, march to the rally, then into the bus with you."

It was easy to hide from the police in the Cafe Lira, which was alongside the square. Then, such happenings were more entertaining than frightening. One could also just as easily leave the precinct.

Then the Democrats came into their own. The Cafe Lira building was knocked down and McDonald's was erected in its place. Now, "Drink Coca-Cola" in gigantic neon looms over the square every night.

The composition of the crowds in the square also changed. Rallies became less frequent. OMON hardly bothered to show up, having been replaced by members of the local 108th Precinct and by sellers of pornography. Beggars made their appearance, as did street musicians playing non-stop and often poorly, and of course, racketeers. It reminded one of society's collapse in the Civil War period (1918-1921). In fact, most of the tunes the musicians played were from that era. It was not so much a matter of nostalgia as of choosing something that suited the atmosphere.

The type of newspaper sold on Pushka also gradually changed. At first, the press of the opposition—excluding a few leftist publications—had concentrated on anticommunism and sang the praises of capitalism. But by the beginning of 1990, the official newspapers, many of which were, as before, the official organs of the Communist party, had started to publish this sort of stuff themselves. Nor was printing articles glorifying the Russian monarchy any longer the sole province of the samizdat.

So the independent press switched to praising Yeltsin and putting down Gorbachev. The official publications, sensing the change in demand, also began to criticize the president of the USSR and laud the leader of Russia. The last hope of the independent press was sex. Pushkin Square was overrun with erotic tabloids and sleazy magazines. One publication was titled simply *The Erotic Gazette*, another *Erotica and Sex*. These titles had a curiously familiar ring: they were reminiscent of such Soviet publications as *Teachers' Gazette*, *Economic Gazette*, and *Hunting and Fishing*. The photos in these publications left a lot to be desired—had someone taken the initiative to import and sell at reasonable prices the more professionally produced porn from the West, such a person would have put the new publishers out of business. It was the trash-publishers' good fortune, therefore, that customs officials were, in their concern for our moral well-being, still confiscating such imports. After August 1992, when authentic Western pornography finally reached Pushka, its prices were so high that few people ended up buying it. The vendors found a way out by charging about five rubles (approximately half of the average daily wage) a peek. Such a gimmick wouldn't have been very successful with the domestic publications because they were, quite simply, un-erotic. At this point, *Tema* newspaper came into its own. Once the demand for "ordinary" erotic literature began to fall, it was able to boost its readership by publishing stories of homosexuality, necrophilia, and bestiality. Of little concern in Moscow in 1990 were the actual living concerns of gays and lesbians.

The breakdown in city government provided a nourishing environment for corruption and crime. In the summer and fall of 1990, I published several articles summing up my thoughts about what was going on in the City Council. To my astonishment, there was hardly any response—at first. It was only after I had given an interview to Radio Liberty where I expressed my feelings about Gavriil Popov did his supporters express offense. It would seem, then, that general questions of urban management were of less interest to the authorities than the issue of who was to be in charge of the city.

I was asked, therefore, why I was writing all this. Didn't I know that I was only pouring salt on the wounds? After all, the other deputies knew just as well as I did about the Council's constant failures but didn't air them in public so as not to give the communists cause to gloat. "Criticizing the new Councils means playing into the hands of party leaders." "Whoever criticizes DemRossiya is providing grist to the CPSU's mill." "Whoever is not with us is against us." These were the sort of remarks I was constantly hearing. Each time, I had to patiently explain to everyone who was ready to listen that there were such stubborn things as facts, that citizens had the right to know the truth, and that until the Democrats understood that they had no monopoly on the truth and that no one should be immune from criticisms, we wouldn't achieve a genuine democracy.

It was vital that the whole truth be told now, before it was too late. Before the voters themselves threw it in our faces along with the reproach that we hadn't justified their faith in us. Or before someone said, "It was better under the old regime."

But my purpose in writing those articles wasn't simply to bolster the principle of free speech. For the Council's weaknesses could only be overcome when effective administrative and municipal reforms were carried out. Already in the spring of 1990, an outline of such reforms appeared to be taking shape in deputies' speeches, in behind-the-scenes discussions, and in some of Gavriil Popov's announcements. The system of urban management had to be reorganized and simplified.

It seemed to us that instead of three dozen or so small district councils, the capital needed nine or ten municipal zones invested with real power and responsibility. Administrative functions could be transferred to the municipal councils. Moscow City Council should be much smaller (a maximum of 150 deputies), with a single executive organ—the coexistence of the ispolkom and presidium was a pointless and unprecedented bureaucratic game.

It is painfully clear that the 1990 new-style district councils were a transitory phenomenon and, as such, were doomed to be ineffective. But did this mean that the faster they disappeared, the better it was? Unfortunately, no.

For all their disastrous shortcomings, City Council and the district councils were the only representative bodies expressing the will of the Muscovites. The shortcomings of the councils were a reflection of the shortcomings and vices of society itself. And clumsy surgery on these councils was akin to experiments on a living organism: mistakes might not be so correctable.

The chief risk of municipal reform was that, in the process, the city might end up without any councils at all, without any representative bodies, in other words without democracy of any sort. Muscovites might find themselves at the mercy of a new, arbitrary executive power. There would be no guarantee that the latter would be any more competent than the old councils.

Reform of the councils was unavoidable, but it should have been undertaken cautiously and only from "below," from within the councils themselves. The same applied to the district authorities. The ground had to be prepared for new elections— on a real multiparty basis. The voters had to be given the chance to vote, not just for "good guys" but for alternative party policies for city and district development.

In short, Moscow needed fundamental, realistic reform in the its administrative structure. But did the city's leaders want this? Popov and Stankevich made it quite clear that what they wanted was stronger executive power, not a more effective Council. Thus, only the City Council deputies themselves could save the day. Would the four hundred or so people chosen by Muscovites to represent their interests, be up to the job? Or would they stop before the precipice?

6

LATE IN AUGUST 1990, I was invited to a conference given by the American Political Science Association in San Francisco. Upon my return, I was to find a fairly bizarre state of affairs at the Mossoviet.

The upper floors of the building had become the headquarters of an anti-crisis squad, in which my socialist colleagues played first violin. Naturally, Yury Luzhkov was in charge of the squad, but Aleksandr Popov had been appointed his deputy. Along with Mikhail Khramov, they had taken over Room N616, turning it into a center of intense and at times fairly chaotic "anti-crisis" activity. The city had run out of cigarettes, and bread deliveries were irregular.

The crisis had long been brewing, and we had warned Stankevich. The situation at the Moscow yeast plant, without which it was impossible to bake bread for the city, had already been catastrophic back in the spring—not only because of old machinery and hold-ups with deliveries of raw materials, but also as a result of bitter antagonism between workers and management. We had tried to get the Council leadership to intervene, but Stankevich had simply brushed us aside. It was only when the first riots started that many people on the Council realized how important it was to ensure the regular supplies of all essential goods to the city.

Convinced that all the city's (and country's) troubles were due to the Communists, the democratic deputies genuinely believed that all they had to do was to undermine the CPSU's position in the capital, after which matters would take care of themselves. In fact, the CPSU's position had been so thoroughly undermined that lots of party functionaries had transferred to commercial firms and joint enterprises. The situation, however, had continued to deteriorate. The city authorities proceeded to blame everything on "Communist saboteurs," and, instead of coming to grips with economic issues, began an inspired battle against sabotage. Results weren't long in coming.

When the Yava tobacco factory closed down for repairs, the city was left without cigarettes, and crowds of angry smokers surged out onto the streets and began to loot the few cigarette kiosks where some packs could still be found. When astonished passerbys asked what was going on, the looters' answered: "Privatizing cigarettes." The Moscow hooligans must be given their due: they understood the essence of privatization a lot faster than did many Ph.D.'s.

Everyone "privatized" whatever and however possible. When Aleksandr Popov, in his capacity as City Council commissar, appeared at the Moscow tobacco factory in order to try and find out just what was going on there, he discovered that the goods were being dispatched in the normal way, but that instead of being delivered to the city's tobacco kiosks they were going somewhere else. "Communist saboteurs" had nothing to do with it. It was a case of the usual brazen thieving. Having mistaken Popov for a client and explained to him what was underway, the packers promised him that as long as he did everything according to the rules, he too could receive several hundred cases of cigarettes. Popov immediately wrote a report and sent it to Luzhkov. As might have been expected, no action was forthcoming, the document being filed in the Council archives.

The riots had to be quelled. This was done by the socialists. To the deputies' general amazement, despite their constant confrontations in the assembly hall, the socialist group worked fairly effectively with Luzhkov during the crisis. This is easily explained. Luzhkov didn't have the slightest sympathy for the socialists, nor it goes without saying, did we for him. But the socialists were capable of working in an energetic and disciplined manner, we didn't take bribes, and we were quick to make contact with people. In a situation like this, when a crisis had to be overcome at any cost, the Council bosses had no other option.

When I first went up to room N616, Yury Khramov came flying past me, talking with someone on a walkie-talkie. Instead of his usual suit, he wore an athletic jacket, under which I saw a bulletproof vest. The person at the other end was yelling about some new problems and Khramov, without stopping to let me know what was going on, rushed on down the stairs.

"Why the bulletproof vest?" I asked one of the members of the legal affairs commission as he tore past me after Khramov.

"What do you mean, why? What if they beat us up?" Kondratiev clarified the situation: "There are three hands now on the levers of power. One of them is ours." Although I was sincerely happy for my fellow deputies, I thought to myself: We won't get far like this.

The bulletproof vests, as it turned out, had their uses. Khramov, along with detachments of OMON, which not long before had dispersed out demonstrations on Pushkin Square, was trying to stop the looting. They went with trucks loaded with cigarettes to the trouble spots. This was somewhat risky. One time, a truck plowed right through the crowd, knocking down some traffic lights as it went. The police, standing alongside, observed what was going on without taking part.

It wasn't just cigarettes that the people looting the kiosks were after. When the trucks arrived, it often turned out that people weren't really interested in the tobacco. There were frequently Stalinist agitators at work among the looters. Arguing with them, standing in the middle of an angry crowd, one often risked serious unpleasantness. Nonetheless, the tobacco crisis was overcome.

Convoys of trucks arrived in Moscow, bringing tobacco from other parts of the country and from Bulgaria. And Gavriil Popov remained true to form by introducing coupons for cigarettes while organizing commercial trade in these goods at truly astounding prices. The money made from the "commercial" sale of cigarettes, it was decided, would go to the Fund for Social Welfare. Within a few months, it became clear that the Fund's finances were not being solely used for Muscovites' social welfare. The money had been deposited for some reason in a commercial bank belonging to the Russian Raw Materials Commodities Exchange and was accruing interest. But this was later. For the moment, Muscovites were celebrating their delivery from the crisis while awaiting the next one.

In summer of 1990, the rumors of an imminent military coup, which had been circulating in Moscow from the very beginning of perestroika, began to seem considerably more likely. Particularly since, given the existing chaos, it had become a real possibility that the power structure itself would organize the coup.

The emergency powers which the USSR Supreme Soviet had twice given Gorbachev remained on paper. This meant that, for the first time in our history, the state actually seemed less powerful and less dictatorial than the law allowed. This inevitably aroused a desire in government circles to "rectify" the situation and to affirm the supremacy of the law. To do so without resorting to force and repression was impossible.

Everyone realized that things couldn't go on like this for long, that something was bound to happen. But nothing did. This uncertainty, and the constant expectation of catastrophe, made the situation intolerably tense.

Each passing day, indeed, provided new cause for alarm. Not far from the Mossoviet, a somewhat bizarre office had appeared, in and out of which people with a military bearing, although dressed in civilian clothes, constantly scurried. Some alert deputies, who had done their military service, noticed a high-frequency antenna there, along with other equipment not usually found in ordinary civilian offices. Where it had come from was anyone's guess. One could have dismissed their reports as paranoia had one's worst suspicions not been borne out by documents.

On October 25, at the entrance to the Mossoviet, I came across an old acquaintance from the Moscow Popular Front, Georgy Guruli.

"Want to see something juicy?" he asked me in a conspiratorial tone.

To be honest, I wasn't particularly interested. I was sure that it was going to be another complaint about infringements of election procedures or petty abuse of power by bureaucrats at the district level. The Council received hundreds of such complaints, and it was impossible to do anything about them since they constituted the norm at all levels of power. However, as I had to wait for someone there anyway, I couldn't avoid taking the document Georgy was holding out to me. I read it and was stunned.

It was a copy of a directive detailing actions to be taken in a "state of emergency," which had been distributed to all the city's gas stations. It instructed that as soon as the code signal "Romanticism 938" was received, only those means of transport with a mobilization order (a sample of which was attached in a separate envelope) were to be filled up. The rest of the document was in the same vein. It was signed by "A. G. Lapshinikov, deputy director of MPKA." The managers of the stations were to sign the directive to confirm that they were acquainted with its contents.

I asked Guruli to take the directive to Yury Khramov's anti-crisis headquarters. It was not the only directive to end up in our hands. By the time Georgy Guruli reached Room N616, quite a lot had come to light.

There had been a report in *Moskovsky Komsomolets* about some strange directives. Some of the deputies began to panic. In Western embassies, by all accounts, they feared the worst. At this point, however, there was no real danger of a coup. For something of the sort to happen, the atmosphere in the capital and in the country as a whole would have to become even more inflamed. For the time being, the professionals were simply resolving their technical problems and preparing for a day which might or might not come.

Naturally, the arrival of a great number of tanks, guns, and even strategic missiles in Moscow, in connection with the anniversary celebrations of the October revolution, only added fuel to the fire. "If the tanks enter the town, they'll never leave," one of the district council leaders told me, clearly agonized. Such statements didn't convince me—if Gorbachev and his inner circle had really been planning a coup, they certainly wouldn't have timed it to coincide with the anniversary of the Bolshevik revolution. As for the military themselves, they would have been unable to contemplate such a move until they had decided what they were going to do afterwards with Gorbachev, Yeltsin, and numerous other officials.

On November 7, 1990, at Red Square, the military parade and the official demonstration in honor of the October revolution proceeded as usual, although one couldn't help thinking that this might be the last of such celebrations.

Before the holiday, the mood among the Democrats came close to panic. Many said that just one determined officer with a platoon of soldiers was all that was needed to seize power and dissolve the Russian government. (Someone noted dryly that the bureaucracy was so bloated, a battalion would be required.)

The rehearsals for the military parade, which, as usual, were held in the capital before the holiday, were this time accompanied by a scandal. Deputy Osovtsov, along with former Yeltsin aide Lev Shimaev, tried to stop the tanks at the entrance to Red Square. Eyewitnesses give different accounts of what exactly took place. Some talk of the civic spirit shown by the deputy who tried to block the path of these formidable machines. Others call it a shameful farce.

According to a member of a tank crew who observed the incident through his vision slit, it all happened on the spur of the moment. "I saw a group of men and women running across the road. They all got across, only one didn't make it. We braked and suddenly he stopped and made straight for us, his hands outstretched. He was yelling something we couldn't hear. In fact it was complete chaos, what with the noise of the motor and people shouting..."

He also added that the man reeked of alcohol. But that takes some believing, for November 7 was a Communist holiday, and a close comrade-in-arms of Gavriil Popov was hardly likely to have been celebrating it.

As for Shimaev, it seems he managed in all of the confusion to lie in turn under several tanks while simultaneously giving an interview to an Izvestia correspondent.

The parade finally took place. Although there was no military coup, there was some unpleasantness. During the official demonstration, several shots were fired at the leaders' viewing stand. It remained unclear who the target had been, since the leaders of both the Communist Party and the heads of the Democratic councils were standing there side by side. They were able to detain the sniper right away, and although he stated he'd been trying to assassinate Gorbachev, much remained unclear.

Immediately after the celebration, another version of the incident began to circulate among City Council deputies. It was said that in fact there had been two shots, and that the second shot had come from the GUM department store—from the other side of the square, where Gorbachev's bodyguard usually sat. They'd been firing at the mausoleum, not at anyone in particular. Just to stir up fear.

Be that as it may, the people standing at the mausoleum had been seriously frightened before the celebration. Leaders were outfitted with bullet-proof pants and vests just to be on the safe side. They moved with difficulty, hobbling up the steps of the mausoleum under the weight of their armor. Popov was an especially pitiful sight. It was clearly a helpless situation for everyone.

Yeltsin and Popov played strange roles at the ceremony. They started by greeting the Communists marching past them, including Pamyat supporters carrying anti-Semitic signs and Stalinists carrying portraits of the "people's leader," who had managed to worm their way into the columns. Then, having descended from the viewing stand, the rulers of Russia and the capital marched at the head of an alternative demonstration which sported anticommunist banners and portraits of the last tsar of Russia, Nicholas II.

That day, thousands of demonstrators with anti-Communist signs marched through Moscow, demanding that the "Great October" celebration be known henceforth as the day of "Great Sorrow." As usual, there was no unity among the Democrats, and as a result, there were two alternative demonstrations occurring simultaneously. One was headed by the recognized leaders of the new Russian and Moscow administrations: Popov, Yeltsin, and their close associates, including Father Gleb Yakunin who immediately transformed the political demonstration into a religious procession.

Meanwhile the radical Democrats who hadn't received—or hadn't wanted to receive—posts in the new administration, including Tatyana Karyagina, Telman Gdlyan, and Vitaly Urazhtsev, marched at the head of the other demonstration (the alternative to the alternative, as it were). If at the main demonstration most of the banners denounced the Bolshevik terror of seventy years ago, the radicals headed for the streets with concrete demands: "President and USSR Parliament— Out!"

The first alternative demonstration took place at Old Square, where the headquarters of the CPSU Central Committee were located, with the All-Union Leninist Communist Youth League and KGB buildings nearby (the "three monsters of the totalitarian regime," to quote *Kuranty* correspondents). At this rally, Yeltsin as usual criticized Gorbachev and his inner *apparat*, which prevented him bringing prosperity to Russia. Gavriil Popov burst into fiery oratory, urging the people on to great deeds:

> The time has come for each man to rise up and save his country. The most important job is up to you, because it is up to each man to save himself. It's up to you to picket the shops, wholesalers' depots, and station warehouses, and to smash the ring of saboteurs that has been organized around Moscow. It's up to you night and day to control the distribution of foodstuffs and to break the mafia's grip. It's up to you, for your sake, for your

children's sake, to bring order to our city and throw out
the thugs and racketeers.

One might have thought that after such a passionate appeal
for action, the ruler of Moscow would have taken steps to
mobilize the masses. But he didn't. In fact, he didn't do anything
at all. Everything continued as before, and those few people who
turned up on their own initiative at the Mossoviet offering to
help, were met by astonished deputies who didn't know what to
do with them.

It's odd that such fiery words were not followed up by even
symbolic action. The city leadership had never before been
commanded to rouse the masses to fight the mafia. But, even if
only for appearances' sake, public control might have been
organized at a few stores, say, or a group of workers sent to at
least one wholesaler's depot. But the rulers of Moscow didn't
dare to do even this, being as they were overcome by a fear of
their own people.

7

WHILE the Democrats and communists argued over whose rally on November 7 had been bigger, the situation around the country continued to deteriorate. Interethnic conflicts shook the Union and Russia. The economy was in shambles, and prescriptions for prosperity put forward by the rival administrations seemed more like prescriptions for suicide. The president of the USSR and his central *apparat* remained at loggerheads with the Russian parliament and Boris Yeltsin. Muscovites stood in line to buy cigarettes at commercial prices and hunted for salt and matches, which had disappeared from the stores. The older generation recalled the war years and said that then, at least, there had been more order.

Thus, there was little cause for joy, but instead of commemorating the victims of the "Bolshevik Terror" (the ideologues of the new democracy did not utter a word about the White terror), it would have been more to the point to mourn the victims of the existing political anarchy.

Free-market prices rose so precipitously that people with no other source of income than their salaries could only sigh and shake their heads. However, for some sectors of the population, the situation had improved markedly. Although the price of a pack of American cigarettes had already reached twenty-five rubles that fall (about 10 percent of the average monthly wage, or half of the average weekly wage), there was no shortage of customers ready to pay such a price.

Professional politicians clearly belonged to the well-heeled minority. The worse the domestic situation became, the more eloquently they discussed the salvation of the Fatherland. The conflict between Yeltsin and Gorbachev remained front-page news in all the papers. The public followed the battle with sinking hearts. Today they would meet and come to agreement. The next day they'd be at loggerheads again. Then the two sides would again refuse to meet, and the public would await new unpleasantness.

As the Russian saying goes: When the lords come to blows, it bodes ill for the serfs. As ever, folk wisdom seemed to hold true. While Yeltsin and Gorbachev were deciding the fate of Russia, Russia itself was heading for a rendezvous with disaster.

Each attempted to demonstrate that his plan for economic reform made the most sense, while his opponent's plan had no chance of succeeding. Each explained that a realization of his opponent's plan would have disastrous, perhaps even irreparable, consequences for the country. It would appear that each side was absolutely correct in his assessment.

Although there was much talk in the press about the major differences between the Russian concept of transition to a market economy and the central government's plans, it took an expert to explain the gist of these differences, and by no means all experts could. The Russian plan, known as the "500 Days," was indeed more radical in the sense that its authors had given no serious consideration to the social consequences of their proposals. For them, the main thing was to distribute state property as swiftly as possible among the upper reaches of the bureaucracy. The central government was inclined to display a greater degree of restraint. The differences, if any, were tactical, for on questions of goals the two sides were in agreement. Both advocated a rapid sharing out of state property, the introduction of free prices, the elimination of the old system of social guarantees, and the expansion of transnational capital's role in the country's economic life. The conflict between Yeltsin and Gorbachev, and between the republican and central bureaucracies that were respectively aligned with them, was really just a power struggle. Naturally, with many millions to be divided up, the issue of who got how much could not but agitate the leaders of the rival factions. Who was to be in charge of the sharing out of real estate? Who was to establish time limits and rules for privatization? These were important issues for both factions.

It is not surprising, therefore, that Boris Yeltsin and Gavriil Popov, for all the growing friction between them, did everything they could to weaken the position of the central bureaucracy. Enterprises slated for privatization became targets of conflict. The Russian administration attempted to gain possession of them before privatization. The Moscow leadership tried to bring as many enterprises as possible under city control, not to extend the municipal sector, but in order to assume control of privatization later on.

Control over privatization didn't just mean pocketing proceeds from sales. There were more lucrative ways of feathering one's nest. The main thing was to be one of the future property owners. Who would win out—the bureaucrats of the central departments, the officials of the Russian ministries, or the Moscow bosses and the business mafia that was linked to them?

Since neither faction could get the better of the other, reforms were constantly postponed, which was not too disastrous for the country. After all, as subsequent events were to show, the proposed treatment would only make the patient—the Soviet economy—worse. At any rate, the enterprises didn't need new owners drawn from the ranks of the old bureaucracy. They needed major capital to invest in modernization (a measure not envisaged in either program), and the development and renewal of the infrastructure—normal roads and a working telecommunications system. But the rulers of Russia and the capital had too many other interesting plans up their sleeves to occupy themselves with such trivial matters. Also, it was practically impossible to catch them in their offices.

In October 1990, the newspaper *Sovietskaya Rossiya* published a list of the trips abroad Popov and Stankevich had taken. In the course of one year, the ruler of Moscow had managed to visit Germany, Italy (twice), Switzerland, the United States, Greece, Austria (twice), France, and Japan and a trip to Israel was planned for the end of the year. Stankevich had been to the States twice and, in addition to France, Greece, Poland, Sweden, Japan, and Taiwan, he had also visited India, Mexico, and Guatemala.

For the professional or semi-professional politician, travelling became somewhat like a drug. A session would be shifted so that the Council sittings wouldn't interfere with travel plans. Some of these journeys established important contacts for the city, but others just resulted in squandered public funds. There was really no way to find out the purposes of each trip, and no one had any intention of elucidating on the subject.

When, in the fall of 1990, I was in Japan for a conference on the history of the Russian Revolution, its organizers informed me with a smile that Sergei Stankevich had just been in Tokyo. He would have done better not to have gone because his return gave rise to a scandal. Stankevich reprimanded his henchmen for coming to greet him at the airport in a couple of Volgas. Why hadn't they sent a minibus? The next day, photographs of Stankevich's baggage appeared in the press, and his homecoming was reported on television.

It wasn't long before another scandal broke out, this time in connection with a journey Stankevich and his wife had taken to Italy. It transpired that the foreign currency for this trip was made available from City Council funds. Stankevich denied this, but the facts were soon corroborated. The first to raise the alarm was the small neo-Bolshevist newspaper *Molniya* ("Lightning"): it published a report including the serial number of the relevant money order. Those deputies had seen Stankevich as a viable alternative to Popov were thrown into confusion. But worse was to come.

Popov, too, had his problems. He had been unwise enough to go to Taiwan before the City Council's delegation had visited China. Taking umbrage at this slight, the Chinese government retaliated by refusing to sign contracts which Moscow's declining economy needed badly. Moreover, because of their presence in the Far East, Popov and Stankevich were absent from a meeting of representatives of Western capitals in Holland at which aid to Eastern Europe was discussed. Their absence naturally affected the results of the meeting. Thus what mattered was not so much the amounts forked out for the journeys, but the larger costs to the city in international affairs.

When, after decades of being cut off from the outside world, trips abroad became possible for tens of thousands of people, all who were in a position to do so did everything they could to get abroad. Socialists, liberals, Communists, and anticommunists, regardless of whether or not they were expected in the West, were all off somewhere, all overcome by a passion for travelling. In any foreign city one might come across hundreds of our people who, more often than not, were there at government expense. Getting off the train at Kongju, South Korea, I decided that I was most probably one of the first Russians to have been there for many years. Imagine my surprise when, in the local history museum, I came across a total of three Europeans, all of whom were Russians!

In discovering the world, we ourselves became a part of it. We not only looked around us, avidly absorbing impressions which only yesterday seemed totally out of our reach; we also put ourselves on show, our way of thinking, sometimes arousing admiration, sometimes surprise, and sometimes aversion in those with whom we came into contact.

The mafia bosses caught the travelling bug, too. On November 3, 1990, *Pravda* informed its readers that the famous Moscow hardened criminal known in the underworld as "Rolik," with several other big shots in the criminal world, had gone abroad for a vacation and for business negotiations. Apparently, "Rolik" and one of his colleagues had been sent to the Eastern European country in question on City Council business. The paper fulminated against the clerk who had submitted the papers to the Ministry of Foreign Affairs and had gotten the visas, but chose to remain silent about the person whose idea it had been to dispatch the delegation in the first place and the person who had given the go-ahead to the Council's external affairs department to obtain foreign passports for these high-level experts.

At the beginning of the Council's second session, it was discovered that virtually the whole of the presidium and a great part of the ispolkom were due to leave on November 25 for Paris. The Council had paid the tickets, and the session was to be broken off on November 24, despite a great amount of unfinished business. To give Popov and Stankevich their due, it has to be said that they were not included in this delegation, preferring individual tourism: one was planning a trip to Israel, the other to the States.

Aleksandr Popov inquired of Stankevich at a session whether there might not be a link between these trips and the break in the Council's work. After a moment of hesitation, accompanied by sniggering from the hall, Stankevich answered that the trips in question were private ones. Walking away from the mike, Popov turned around and gave the chairman of the Council a low bow.

Thus, no break was made in the session's work. The majority of those on the list for Paris went anyway, but some decided on this occasion not to go. Our leaders, too, decided to cancel their "business" trips abroad. Gavriil Kharitonovich didn't go to Jerusalem as scheduled, while Stankevich continued to chair the Council sittings. Following this incident, relations between Stankevich and the socialists became strained. The socialists realized that although they were free to criticize the political decisions of the ruling circles without arousing any special ire, they had only to touch on the latter's material interests to earn themselves real and implacable enemies. We knew what this meant but were not prepared to give way.

The corruption which reigned in the city and district administrations made normal work virtually impossible, even in those cases where the people at the top tried to introduce order. The new people had not yet managed to line their own pockets, but they very much wanted to do so. They took bribes just as the old guard had done, but were far less competent in solving concrete issues. As a result, even giving bribes was no guarantee of success. The economic managers were at their wits' end. They no longer even knew how big a bribe to give, or to whom and for what it should be given. Managers thought wistfully of the good old days when one bribe was enough to solve any problem. Now they had to give bribes left, right and center, with nothing to show for it.

It wouldn't be right, however, to place all the blame for the corruption on the new personnel. The real Molotov cocktail occurred when the new staff found common cause with the old staff and took over their habits.

When the company Soyuzinterprom offered to build two blocks of flats in the Bauman district of Moscow in exchange for the right to rent 2,500 square meters of non-housing-stock accommodation, the local authorities were unable to come to a decision on the matter. However, via middlemen, Soyuzinterprom was unexpectedly offered a contract for the rental of equivalent accommodation for the modest bribe of no more than 2.8 million rubles. The company's directors turned the offer down, though, since by law bribes of this size incurred the death penalty.

When I heard this story, I wondered why such an odd sum had been named: not 2.5 or 3 million, but 2.8 million. There were two possibilities. Either the sum included the middlemen's commission (in an "extra" 300,000) or somewhere a big privatization scheme was under way with real estate valued at 2.8 million rubles.

If the city's affairs were going badly and the capital's economy was sliding into ever-deepening crisis, the affairs of the city leaders and their private business activities were flourishing. Luzhkov founded and headed a joint-stock company called Orgkomitet (Organizing Committee). Popov set up a joint-stock company possessing considerable capital, with the modest name of The Institute for the Development of Moscow, which received numerous profitable commissions from the city. Stankevich headed the advisory council of Moscow's Biznesbank.

Biznesbank was founded as a commercial bank, part of whose

capital belonged to the city. Or, to be more accurate, the city invested with Biznesbank its own municipal Zhilsotsbank (Housing Bank), along with its buildings, capital, and personnel. The latter turned out to be the least valuable part of the deal and the majority were immediately fired. The rest handed in their notices after a visit from their new boss, Sergei Stankevich. Never before, they said, had they been so rudely spoken to.

News of the Biznesbank scandal broke thanks to the efforts of the ubiquitous *Moscovsky Komsomolets* journalist, Anatoly Baranov, who wrote an article called "The Price of Power." But this wasn't the end of the scandal. According to the *Molniya*, Stankevich took a vacation in France, paid for by a French firm, which, as it became known later, was a Biznesbank partner. Stankevich, we were told, received no salary from the bank. One can only admire the industry of Moscow's second-in-command who, despite the city's numerous problems, also found time to manage a bank and, what is more, on a voluntary basis.

Following the publication of Baranov's article in December 1990, Stankevich made haste to contact the *Moskovsky Komsomolets*'s editor-in-chief, Pavel Gusev. He had no intention of disputing the facts cited in Baranov's article; They were true, only too true! But it was clear to everyone that measures would have to be taken to ensure that nothing of the sort was ever repeated. Baranov was fired and his department at the newspaper reorganized. And thus the problem of the corruption scandals was largely overcome. It was only at first that the division of spheres of influence between the old Communist bureaucracy and the new Democratic oligarchy gave rise to conflict. Already by fall 1990, it was obvious that the two sides were finding common ground. Attacks on the city leadership in the Communist press had almost ceased, and the Democrats, while continuing to rant against the no longer existent totalitarian Communism, refrained from hitting out at specific individuals in the old bureaucracy.

One of the main trophies inherited by the new city bosses was the old propaganda *apparat*. Besides the traditionally liberal press, which publicized the policies of Popov and Yeltsin, the leaders of the Council could always plead their cause to the capital's inhabitants on Moscow television. Gavriil Popov appeared on TV literally every week. Wearing his inevitable dark blue sweater, he talked patiently to Muscovites, like a kind uncle who was genuinely sorry for his muddle-headed relatives who had to have elementary things explained to them over and over. Many liked this.

The opposition, naturally, was not allowed on the air. The Council took over *Vechernyaya Moskva*, to which were added the new shows *Stolitsa* ("The Capital") and *Kuranty*, funded by the City Council and reflecting the point of view of its leaders. The Communist *Moskovskaya Pravda* chose not to challenge the authorities.

The only major newspaper in the capital to stand independent from the power structure on the Council and in the country as a whole, was *Moskovsky Komsomolets*. It didn't take the editors long to discover, moreover, that it was to their independent position that they owed their growing readership.

The more license the newspaper allowed itself, the more often it incurred answering fire from the city leadership. In one of his television appearances, Popov accused *Moskovsky Komsomolets* of disseminating false information. The paper retaliated by publishing new facts on the corruption and incompetence of the city authorities. The conflict became increasingly public, and Muscovites, disappointed by the Democrats' unfulfilled promises, listened to what the paper had to say.

The conflict between *Moskovsky Komsomolets* and the authorities peaked when, in answer to new accusations of unscrupulous and irresponsible conduct from the Council ispolkom, *Moskovsky Komsomolets* published an article stating that, judging by the way things were going, the ispolkom leaders would soon find themselves strung up from the lampposts.

If one considered the mood of the citizens, driven frantic by constantly standing in line, empty stores, and transportation delays, these words might easily have turned out to be prophetic. The authorities had the paper's editor-in-chief, Pavel Gusev, summoned to the public prosecutor's office. Although Gusev was a Council deputy, he stood his ground. It wasn't long before new reports exposing the corruption of the city elite appeared in the pages of his paper.

This time, the journalists selected Karnaukhov as their target. Karnaukhov was in charge of Moscow commerce. Articles on Karnaukhov were given headlines in the style of the *bylina*, the traditional Russian heroic poem. From one issue to the next, Karnaukhov was presented to readers as a great hero—the only difference being that his deeds, instead of doing good, did evil. The first article in the series was called "How Karnaukhov Fed Moscow." Soon a new piece by Anatoly Baranov appeared, with the equally heroic title, "How Karnaukhov Regaled the Workers with Sugar."

For all their *bylina*-like headlines, there was nothing fictional about the content of these articles. They reproduced photocopies of documents and quoted facts which proved beyond any doubt that it was the City Council ispolkom, and not the mysterious dark powers to which Luzhkov and Popov were so fond of alluding, that bore responsibility for the breakdown in the city economy, the corruption, and the shortages.

Moskovsky Komsomolets also published reports on the absolutely routine bureaucratic pasts of the Democrats on the new ispolkom. The city's top brass had preferred to keep quiet of late about the high points of their previous careers. But a group of socialist deputies came to the paper's aid. It took them only a few days to dig up from the Council archives a list of the previous appointments held by the ispolkom members. As was only to be expected, most of them had flourished under Communist totalitarianism, the horrors of which they now so eloquently condemned.

For almost a year, *Moskovsky Komsomolets* was the only truly independent press organ, the only one that spoke the truth regardless of whom it benefitted. It hit out in turn against the CPSU gorkom and the City Council leadership. The enormous popularity the paper enjoyed—it was the biggest city newspaper in the world—made it a very real danger for those in power. It wasn't surprising that the city leaders went all out to try to bring the unruly paper to heel.

With the first attempts to threaten the paper being unsuccessful, the Moscow bosses changed tactics. With telephone calls to the editorial offices, Popov and Gusev began negotiations. It would appear that the negotiations were successful, for the editor-in-chief's behavior underwent an abrupt change. At the paper it was said that Gusev had gone off his head.

After the Biznesbank scandal, Anatoly Baranov was forced to leave the paper. In March 1991 he joined the Socialist Party and was elected a member of its executive committee. *Moskovsky Komsomolets* stopped publishing its exposes of corruption in the city leadership and, by spring 1991, many of the newspaper's articles looked as if they had been dictated in Gavriil Popov's office itself. You can't stop progress.

Having dealt with the Biznesbank scandal, the city rulers turned their attention to new improvements, this time in the fields of architecture and interior decoration. The Council's Department of External Relations was relocated, and reconstruction work began on office accommodations for Stankevich and Popov. Now to the Mossoviet building, which combined (as I have stated before) nineteenth-century Russian classicism with Stalinist pseudo-classicism, were added suites of chambers decorated in—how best to put it?—Popov neo-classicism. But this "Feast during the Plague" must have seemed even to the city bosses themselves somewhat too eye-catching. They only showed their innovations—the new office suites were decorated in mahogany paneling and silk—to a select few.

Right after the decoration work was completed, we began to take small groups of people on guided tours of the new offices, but evidently someone heard of this. On December 7, 1990, I was stopped by three men in plain clothes at the entrance to Popov's chambers. When asked what I was doing there, I answered that I was a Council deputy looking around the Mossoviet building, which I had every right to do. "You can't go in there," I was told. Then, for some reason, they added: "They aren't finished yet." The three men looked like they meant business and, for all my deputy's immunity, I was reluctant to enter into a fight with them.

8

THE SECOND session of the Democratic Moscow City Council opened on November 12, 1990. The first session had to be convened at the House of Political Education, belonging to the Communist Party, for which the Council had paid rent amounting to tens of thousands of rubles. This time, it was decided that we would economize and meet in the Mossoviet's own Marble Hall. The previous spring, the Council ispolkom had told the deputies there wasn't enough room for all of us in the Marble Hall. In November, though, despite the fact there had been no reduction in our numbers, we all managed to fit quite easily.

This was not the only surprise of the second session. At its opening, the majority of deputies, showing a healthy concern for their own skins, voted that the live broadcast of Council proceedings be canceled. From then on, Muscovites would see only those parts of the debates which the television bosses or Council leadership considered appropriate to be shown.

The broadcasts had been stopped, it was said, because they cost central television too much. However, in conversations among themselves, the deputies often gave a completely different explanation. One of them said, "If Muscovites knew everything that went on here, they'd come and blow the Mossoviet up."

Even after the deputies had decided against a full broadcast of the proceedings, someone obviously still found the presence of the TV cameras irksome. During one of the debates, when the presidium was answering some tricky questions posed by people in the back-benches, the power for the TV equipment was suddenly cut off. For some reason it proved impossible either to remedy the problem on the spot or to link up the cameras to the Council power circuit. A new generator had to be ordered from central television which took an unusually long time to arrive.

One of the first to speak at the opening of the second session was deputy Sergei Balashov, who had made a name for himself by his wild behavior at the first session. We couldn't open the second session, he said, because we hadn't closed the first session as was required by parliamentary procedure. This was quite right. The presidium and the assembly were somewhat put out by Balashov's insistence that the first order of business be to close the first session, after which, and only after which, the second session could be convened. They took it as a malicious joke.

"Don't pay any attention to him," someone shouted from the hall. "He'll get bored. Let's get down to work!"

When passions had subsided, and the presidium had regained control, Gavriil Popov took the floor.

Starting off by saying that "our authority is also in the throes of deep crisis," the Council leader proceeded to give a detailed account of plans for privatization of commerce, housing stock, industry, the consumer services, health care, and education, as well as for the introduction of our own "Moscow money" and a rationing system which, in some inexplicable way, would tie in with free trade. When all these measures were eventually put into practice, they'd act as a powerful stimulus to labor and free enterprise. In the meantime, during the transition period, Muscovites would have to tighten their belts: the Moscow authorities were unable to help them, for, alas, "much in the city no longer depends on us...."

He ended on an optimistic note: supplies of fuel and foodstuffs had been laid in. Thus, we were just as well prepared for the winter this time as we had been in previous years. "Those who talk of an unprecedented or extreme crisis," he said, "are those who would like to see such a crisis."

This speech left the deputies in some bewilderment. Was there a crisis in the city, or not? How did an "extreme" crisis differ from an "ordinary" crisis? And how was the absence of foodstuffs in the stores to be explained, if there had been just as many food shipments to the city as usual, and nothing out of the ordinary was going on?

Since it was absolutely pointless putting such questions to Popov (his answers would only add to their confusion), the deputies fairly went on to the debates.

There were three main points of conflict at the session: administrative reform (special status for the capital), the reform of commerce (widespread privatization accompanied by a rationing system), and housing reform (privatization of housing stock).

If the first session was characterized by constant clashes between DemRossiya and the Moscow bloc, this time Dem-Rossiya was virtually non-existent. Its former supporters had split up into a mass of minor fractions and groups. Nor did the Moscow bloc show itself to be particularly active. Meanwhile, a new opposition was formed out of the old DemRossiya members, which caused the city leadership more and more trouble.

Before the start of the second session, a socialist group was officially registered for the first time with the Council. The socialists had set up their party earlier on, in June 1990. What was happening now was the formal unification of the socialist deputies. In order to attract deputies having no particular alignment to their ranks, they decided to call themselves the Moscow Left-Wingers. Vladimir Kondratov was elected leader of the group. It was the youngest group on City Council, and it soon began to act as a united team.

On the initiative of the Moscow Left-Wingers, several opposition groups united at the second session into a new Democratic bloc, a reproduction in miniature of the former DemRossiya. Only this time the enemy was not Communist totalitarianism, which had safely receded into the past, but the new oligarchy, which had rapidly come into being due to the merging of the upper reaches of the Democratic leadership with the old corrupt *apparat*.

United in the new coalition—to their surprise—were not only greens and socialists, who were traditionally close to each other in their ideologies and aims, but also some liberals and Christian Democrats. The formal basis for their cooperation was their common wish to defend democratic values, their insistence on clean politics, and their observance of democratic procedures.

This was an attempt to transform the square wheels of the city's political machine into round ones. There was no agreement, nor could there be, as to which direction we should move, but it was vital to try to save at least those elements of democracy which, to a greater or lesser degree, already existed.

"The democratic norms proclaimed by our right honorable Council leadership have remained at the level of words," said Vladimir Kondratov on the first day of the session, speaking on behalf of the Moscow Left-Wingers. "Instead of organizing the work of the corpus of deputies, the Council presidium has deteriorated into an organ rubber-stamping, in our name, decisions made in secret.

"The constant chain of crises has prompted our leadership to push, behind our backs, the project for administrative reform through the higher echelons of government at republic and Union levels. We consider that if the bill for special status for the city is passed it will result in a totalitarian regime of administration by that same incompetent leadership and will put an end to all democratic reform for the next few years."

It is obvious that democracy was a hindrance to the political plans of many highly-placed Democrats. Back in August, Gavriil Popov had published an article in the *New York Review of Books* under the telling title, "The Dangers of Democracy." In this American paper, the ruler of the Soviet capital had convincingly argued that, in Russia, democratic freedoms were the main obstacle to the introduction of market capitalism.

Popov and Stankevich had said more than once before the session opened that the Council was incapable of working effectively. The chairman of Lensoviet, Anatoly Sobchak, had openly demanded that Lensoviet be abolished and a new authoritarian regime be introduced in Leningrad and the country overall. The new oppositionists, however, believed that the Council, for all its operetta-like image and incapacity for effective work, represented a barrier to the appearance of a new authoritarianism.

The new opposition bloc showed itself capable of acting in a united front on many economic issues, too. Taking the Council presidium by surprise, some liberal deputies supported the socialists in their criticism of the privatization projects. The subtle position adopted by the Moscow Left-Wingers, who declared that we were ready in some cases to support privatization—provided that all the norms of financial control existing in "civilized countries" were scrupulously observed—brought its rewards. As was only to be expected, the Council leadership could not agree to this. The acceptance of such conditions would have undermined the whole privatization program. First, it would take years to ensure public control over privatization and a more or less objective assessment of the real cost of the property to be privatized, and to draft appropriate legislation and establish a mechanism to enforce it. Second, the corrupt bureaucracy, which at the time, was the only serious contender for privatized property, simply could not and would not acquire it according to "civilized" rules. The only privatization mechanism viable under the circumstances was to distribute the property according to the old bureaucratic rules. Those who had done well under the old regime stood to do even better under the new.

The idealistic liberals who dreamed of civilized capitalism, "as in the West," protested as they saw incipient Russian capitalism acquire increasingly ugly traits. These protests didn't achieve anything, which is not surprising: liberals' inability to accomplish the goals they set for themselves is a fact of life in our country. Idealistic liberals in Russia, for the most part decent although naive people who are taken in by the mass media, set themselves unrealistic goals and are therefore unable to find fitting means for their realization.

The socialists, on the contrary, were deeply convinced that, given the circumstances, only an ugly and authoritarian capitalism was possible. Therefore, there was nothing particularly surprising for us in what was going on. It may be paradoxical, but if there was anyone on the Council who really understood Gavriil Popov, it was the Moscow Left-Wingers.

Serious politicians in the Russian and Moscow leadership were just as aware as the leftist opposition that capitalism in Russia would take monstrous and savage forms, although they were reluctant to admit this in public. The privatization debates in the Council made this so obvious that the authorities had to resort to censorship. Most of the speeches made by the Moscow Left-Wingers in the privatization debates were not shown on television.

Nevertheless, the situation remained on the whole under the control of the presidium. The project of achieving special status for the city, which Popov discussed with Gorbachev and Yeltsin without the participation of the deputies, was not submitted for discussion at the session. The project for ration cards for Moscow ran into strong opposition when the deputies found out that the food quotas would only be a little more generous than those in force during the war in blockaded Leningrad, while all the surplus foodstuffs would be sold off at commercial prices. The project for housing privatization supported by the presidium likewise met with a cool reception from the majority of deputies, who put forward an alternative project.

The presidium's control over the deputies was slowly weakening, while the deputies were beginning to acquire an ability for independent assessment and action. But less and less hope remained that we would have a chance to show it.

Even such a mundane task as the duplication of session documents was made difficult for the opposition. Such problems were, however, surmountable. What was more difficult was to let other citizens know what was going on in the Red House. The screening of the debates on television, which thousands of Muscovites watched, was organized in such a way as to give peak viewing time to Gavriil Popov. The speeches of the opposi tion were shown late at night by which time most people had gone to bed.

While we sat in session, the real authorities discussed a variety of projects for administrative reform, all of which reduced to nil the role of the elected organs. The Muscovites lost all trust in the deputies, who appeared to be unable to solve a single issue.

As it became more and more obvious that administrative reform was inevitable, the conflict between city and district authorities became worse. The clash between the city leadership and the urban districts had started back in summer 1990 when Democratic euphoria had been at its peak. In some places, even the sovereignty of the urban district had been discussed, and the Krasnopresnensky district council had scared the whole world by declaring that it intended to assert sovereignty over its air space and to charge foreign aircraft flying through it a duty payable in foreign currency.

Ilya Zaslavsky, the leader of the Oktyabrsky district council, announced it was his aim to "build capitalism in one district on its own." What this meant in practice was that Zaslavsky and his inner circle made use of their new position in order to become capitalists themselves as quickly as possible. Numerous firms were set up at municipal expense, which were headed by the district leaders. Privatization of district real estate began, although sale proceeds did not appear in the budget. A series of shocking scandals followed, and the deputies of the district council demanded that Zaslavsky step down. This, however, was not easy to accomplish. Although the overwhelming majority of deputies voted for Zaslavsky's replacement, the chairman of the council and his supporters just wouldn't turn up at a sitting. As a result, each time, they came a few votes short of a quorum. For several months the council was paralyzed, while the looting of municipal funds continued.

Pykhtin attempted to reform local government in the Cheremushki district of Moscow by cutting down the administrative staff and uniting the posts of council chairman and leader of the ispolkom. This ended in a blockade of the

Cheremushki district by the city leadership, which did not agree to such reform.

The reforms Pykhtin introduced gave a powerful boost to democracy at district level by setting up a strong, effective, and authoritative district administration. This obviously did not accord with Luzhkov and Popov's plans. The latter made no secret of the fact that their aim was not to reform the district councils but to abolish them. This would enable them to concentrate power and real estate in their own hands, to dispose of as they saw fit.

Aware of this danger, the majority of district councils set up a coordinating center, in which Pykhtin played one of the key roles. However, matters didn't proceed beyond general discussions and protests against the illegal actions of the city authorities. The city and district deputies themselves became increasingly skeptical. Many openly discussed what they would do when the councils were dissolved.

Sometimes it seemed there would be no need even to disperse the deputies. In the middle of the second session we were all nearly eaten alive. The city leadership, in an effort to cut down on the consumption of foodstuffs, ordered that no meat from state funds be allocated to animals in circuses and zoos. At first the circus performers were nonplussed, but then the famous actor and clown Yury Nikulin came up with an original solution. He announced it to the media, and the whole country got to hear of it:

> Tomorrow we will all work as usual. On Friday we will cancel all performances, and on Saturday we'll load up the circus trailers with the tigers in their cages and placards, hop aboard ourselves, and drive to the Mossoviet. We'll go regardless of whether or not our action is approved. And if they resort to force to disperse us, we'll open the cages.

It's quite possible that deputies being devoured alive in public by beasts of prey was just the sort of spectacle Muscovites longed to see. But tigers, even tame tigers, are illiterate, so they would have been unable to determine who was responsible for drafting and signing which documents. As is customary in Rus, they'd have ended up eating the wrong people, after which they would have had to apologize.

9

AT THE BEGINNING of November, despite the new opposition, it was clear that the Council leadership was firmly in control of the session. Even the deputies' obvious reluctance to accept the official projects for privatization of housing and commerce in their original form did not pose too much of a threat to the presidium, which continued regardless to pursue its own policy without bothering to consult with the deputies.

The "bomb" went off on Friday, November 26, just when the city fathers were congratulating themselves on a victory: their project for the reform of nursery school education, which was unanimously opposed by nursery school teachers, had been passed by a majority vote. Everything seemed to be going fine until the chairman of the legal affairs commission, Yury Petrovich Sedykh-Bondarenko, mounted the podium and demanded the immediate resignation of General Bogdanov, the chief of the Moscow GUVD. A new candidate for the post, already approved by the commission, was immediately put forward: General Komissarov.

This was not just a re-shuffle of personnel.

It's obvious that, in conditions of permanent political crisis, all factions had an interest in who was to be chief of police for the city. But Bogdanov and Komissarov were important figures in their own right.

During his term as first secretary of the CPSU Moscow

gorkom, Boris Yeltsin had appointed Bogdanov. Bogdanov had remained on good terms with Yeltsin's successors, too. A member of the Moscow police force said something that could explain this: namely, that his boss never made public any matter or document which could harm influential people. Neither the liberal camp gathered around Yeltsin and Popov, nor their adversaries from the CPSU gorkom, were anxious to lose such an accommodating person. Especially since, if forced to leave, the general could make trouble if he wanted to. Thus, as was only to be expected, the Moscow group and the Council leadership were adamantly opposed to Sedykh-Bondarenko's proposal.

Komissarov, moreover, well known for his fight against the mafia, was the direct opposite of Bondarenko. His career to date hadn't been very successful, due mainly to a strange reluctance on his part to protect the reputations of the highly placed. In addition, Komissarov had just applied for the position of Russian minister of Internal Affairs in Yeltsin's administration and had been turned down. Appointing such a figure as chief of the Moscow GUVD would not bode well for either CPSU politicians or the leaders of the Democrats.

The debate became heated. Just when the radical deputies were beginning to gain the upper hand, demanding that the issue be put to a vote, Stankevich, who had been absent all day, suddenly appeared in the hall from God knows where and took over chairmanship of the meeting. This didn't help, however: the mutiny from within the Democratic majority was an accomplished fact.

The shouts and general uproar, usual at Council sittings, now surpassed anything that had been seen thus far. Trying to establish control, Stankevich found himself more and more embroiled in conflict with the floor. Having learned of Bogdanov's insulting refusal to meet with the legal affairs commission, the deputies were out for blood. Many of the "backbenchers" had their own accounts to settle with the chief of the Moscow police. Some had been arrested during demonstrations; others had been beaten up.

Komissarov's speech may not have been a great feat of oratory, but it testified to his professional competence. The outcome of the fight appeared to be a foregone conclusion.

Stankevich managed only to prolong the sitting. We can't, he argued, take a decision in Yury Luzhkov's absence. Sedykh-Bondarenko reminded those present that Luzhkov had been informed of the commission's decision on November 5, but had not considered it necessary to take any action. His words were drowned in the general hubbub.

Eventually, Luzhkov mounted the rostrum. He said he would speak for no longer than one minute, and he kept his word. The speech of the city's chief apparatchik may be reduced to a simple formula:

> I appoint the chief of police. If he has to be fired, the timing is up to me. If a change of appointment has to be made, I decide who the new man is to be. It is my team and City Council had best not poke its nose where it is not wanted.

In a way Luzhkov was right. By interfering in personnel matters, City Council was curtailing the executive power, perhaps paralyzing it. However, Luzhkov's power was, in fact, urgently in need of curtailment.

Luzhkov's speech, with its concealed threat against the Council, was hardly likely to win him popularity with the deputies. But this wasn't what he was after. He probably expected it to make the deputies stop to think; he thought perhaps that, having realized they were provoking a crisis, they would take fright. However, this didn't happen. The atmosphere wasn't conducive to analytic reflection.

The hall voted.

When the ballot boxes were opened, it was discovered that the Council had voted by an overwhelming majority for Bogdanov's removal and Komissarov's appointment in his place.

On the evening of the following day it became known that Luzhkov had handed in his resignation.

Panic set in among the deputies. It was clear that Luzhkov's resignation would lead inevitably to Popov's downfall.

Meanwhile the outcome of the fight still hung in the air, because as of Friday evening the victorious majority hadn't managed to get the results of the secret ballot confirmed. Now this procedure, usually a formality, was at the center of a real political battle.

Standing at the doors of the Mossoviet on Monday morning were picketers from Zelenograd, activists from the independent trade union of uniformed police, and women who not long before had shouted slogans in support of Popov at the Democrats' meetings. Now they held placards demanding that Komissarov be immediately confirmed in his appointment, and shouted curses against Popov and Stankevich.

On Monday morning, the sitting was opened by Gavriil Popov, who threatened that, should the results of the voting be confirmed, he would resign. He reminded the deputies of the infringements of procedure that had occurred (it seems to me that without such infringements, it was impossible to get resolutions passed in the Council). He also drew their attention to the fact that on Friday, deputy Ivanov from the legal affairs commission had said that Komissarov had Yeltsin's support. This statement did not correspond to the facts; the deputies had been misinformed.

Popov threatened to hold an inquiry, and some deputies even thought that he intended to have Ivanov put in prison. Appearing in the hall later on, Russian Parliament deputy Rebrikov told those present that he had come across Gavriil Popov by chance in Yeltsin's outer office, where the ruler of Moscow had turned up with the prepared text of a letter. In this letter, Yeltsin was to publicly pronounce anathema on Ivanov and to dissociate himself from Komissarov. Rebrikov maintained that he himself succeeded in persuading Yeltsin not to sign the letter.

Yeltsin didn't sign any letter, preferring, as always, to keep aloof. But the "chance" appearance of Rebrikov in Yeltsin's outer office at such a crucial moment was reminiscent of a scene from a play in which the hero, wanting to perform a serenade, quite unexpectedly comes across a piano in the bushes. Rebrikov belonged to the Gdlyan group, and it was no secret that this group supported Komissarov. Also, members of the Gdlyan group had somehow managed to get into the hall, to which admittance was by pass only, and were attentively following the course of events.

Ponomaryov, the public prosecutor, also turned up at the Mossoviet and told the deputies that General Bogdanov had been illegally dismissed and that he, in his capacity as prosecutor, would defend the rights of the injured party.

Passions flared. Popov had made his speech. Without opening the debates, the chairman of the Council announced a break in the proceedings and left the hall. A few dozen of his supporters obediently followed in their master's wake.

For all practical purposes, the sitting had been broken off, for there was no quorum. Although according to Council regulations, the chairman should have consulted with the deputies before announcing a break in the proceedings, there was nothing anyone could do about it. Those deputies who remained in the hall attempted to continue the debate, but it proved impossible to work normally. Eventually, the deputies dispersed to their fractional meetings, while only those Democrats remained in the hall who, not being aligned to any particular fraction and for want of anything better to do, stood there arguing vociferously.

Right then, the police appeared in the hall with a huge dog and requested the deputies to vacate the premises because, they said, there had been a bomb scare.

Failing to find a real bomb, the dog and its escort withdrew. As always on such occasions, not one of the many journalists who were milling about the assembly hall that day managed to get a photo of the dog. The photographers kicked themselves, their only consolation being that their rivals hadn't managed to, either. That evening, having found a briefcase in the deputies' room and suspecting that this might be the famous bomb, they were about to call the police, when Vladimir Kondratov turned up and took possession of his case.

A political bomb nearly went off. The city authorities let it be understood that they were scared by Komissarov's appointment.

In so doing, they indirectly confirmed the accusations of corruption that had been brought against them. However, it was still too early for the opposition to celebrate. Neither Popov nor Luzhkov intended to give way, particularly since concessions over the Komissarov affair might cost them too dearly.

Reopening the Council meeting following the unplanned break in the proceedings, Gavriil Kharitonovich deceived the deputies yet again by not allowing the faction representatives to speak as had been promised. Instead, it was suggested that those wishing to speak on "the theme of the vote" should make use of the mikes in the hall.

Towards evening, by which time everyone was totally exhausted, "a vote by name to confirm the results of the secret ballot" was announced. It was clear that those deputies who were members of the police force and who had voted against their boss in the secret ballot would abstain this time. Behind-the-scenes lobbying of individual deputies by members of the presidium also produced results: a number of deputies left before the voting started.

Thus, when the name vote was counted, 170 deputies had voted for confirmation of the results of the secret ballot, and 134 against. The rest had either not taken part in the voting or had abstained. Popov and Stankevich remained in the minority, but the opposing faction had not achieved its goal since 170 votes was not sufficient to confirm Komissarov's appointment. Neither side had obtained a majority; thus, Bogdanov remained in his post, and Popov, Luzhkov, and Stankevich were free to continue their activities.

When the session secretariat made public the results of the name vote, it became clear who had saved Gavriil Popov. The CPSU group had voted cordially with the Democratic presidium against confirmation of the results of the secret ballot. Their common interest in saving Bogdanov was obvious. The Communists were out to save their man; the new rulers didn't want Komissarov. There was, incidentally, another explanation: neither faction wanted Komissarov since both of them were stealing.

Having blocked Komissarov's appointment, the members of the presidium calmed down somewhat, although the battle over the GUVD continued. It was clear that, in view of what had occurred, Bogdanov would sooner or later have to go anyway. The question was, who would replace him?

The deputies were addressed by chief of the Moscow OBKhSS (our remarkable police division that battles embezzlement and speculation) Shestopalov, by all accounts one of the presidium's key candidates for chief of police. However, Shestopalov's meeting with the deputies was accompanied by a new scandal. Aleksandr Popov appeared at the mike and told those present that while Shestopalov had been in charge of the division a list of the secret OBKhSS agents had in some mysterious way ended up "by mistake" at Moscow City Inquiries. Information from the Ministry of Internal Affairs Zonal Information Center was now concentrated in their hands, and now, by dialing 019, members of the mafia and other interested parties could check, just for a few kopecks as was entirely in keeping with the spirit of the laws of the free market, whether a particular suspicious-looking type might not be a secret OBKhSS agent. A full list could also be obtained if one so wished.

Information, of course, is a salable commodity, but never before had such valuable information been available so cheaply.

Shestopalov was somewhat taken aback by Popov's accusation. After a pause, he said:

"But none of our agents has suffered!"

The Council legal affairs commission, having staked everything on Komissarov, didn't give up the fight. Nor did the other side yield, although it engaged in a series of sneaky maneuvers. Luzhkov put forward his scenario for a solution in which Komissarov, without being asked, was allocated the role of deputy chief of the GUVD. Komissarov and his supporters turned down this compromise, but their position was complicated by the fact that Yeltsin gave his undivided support to Luzhkov. The majority of the members of the legal affairs commission were reluctant to be seen as going against Tsar Boris. In their public statements, the deputies were inclined to keep to the traditional formula "the tsar is good, it is the boyars who are bad," arguing that the good and magnanimous Yeltsin had simply been misled by Popov and Luzhkov, although Yeltsin personally was in control of the course of events and carefully followed everything that took place in the capital.

While the legal affairs commission was waging a war for justice, all the other commissions were simply collapsing. They all suffered from a common defect: the absence of a quorum. To get deputies to attend meetings was virtually impossible, especially since many of them already realized that the commissions were powerless to make any important decisions. As the commissions turned into arenas for self-expression by incompetent amateurs, their few professional members gradually lost interest in such gatherings. The result was a vicious circle: the more empty chatter there was, and the more personal ambition raised its head at commission meetings, the less often serious politicians attended. And the fewer the experts present, the more empty chatter there was. Whenever it did prove possible to summon a quorum, there were unexpected results. The commission on commerce, having gathered together half its members, voted in a new chairman by a small majority of votes. The chairman's supporters retaliated by threatening to call a new meeting, with a different composition of members, and to put the issue to the vote again. Since one or two votes were decisive, this game of leapfrog could go on forever.

Ironically, due to the Komissarov affair, the legal affairs commission was the most united and hardworking of these bodies, although its actual achievements were next to nil. The conflict over Komissarov continued—now dying down, now flaring up again—over the course of several months. Most of the deputies, like most Muscovites, were gradually losing interest in the battle. It became obvious that, whatever the outcome might be, it was no use expecting significant changes. The opportunity to achieve a change in the alignment of forces within the GUVD had been lost. But for the legal affairs commission, the appointment of Komissarov had become a matter of honor.

In November, General Bogdanov had reported sick and promised to step down, asking only for honorary retirement (playing for time in order to organize the appointment of a suitable successor); now, he suddenly got better and declared that he had no intention of leaving and had never mentioned retiring. Bogdanov's statement had even Luzhkov nonplussed; in November, Luzhkov had appealed to the deputies to take pity on the poor, sick general. Luzhkov sent Bogdanov a sharply-worded letter. The correspondence between Bogdanov and Luzhkov ended up in the press, completely mystifying the public.

Eventually, the issue of who was to be chief of police was actually put to a vote once again. The Council voted for Komissarov. But this time, too, the legal affairs commission was out of luck. The Council resolution was challenged by the Ministry for Internal Affairs.

Humiliated by their defeat, and convinced now that City Council had no power whatsoever, the members of the commission resorted to an extreme and unexpected move. At the end of March, the commission announced it was going on a hunger strike.

The hunger strike took place in the Russian Supreme Soviet building. It was a bizarre spectacle, with both tragic and comic aspects. The deputies sat unshaven, tormented by hunger, wearing their suits and City Council badges. Here, too, were cots and blankets. Since there was a permanent quorum, the commission met virtually non-stop. Reports were delivered, and resolutions passed. Functionaries and deputies of the Russian Supreme Soviet walked by preoccupied with their own problems, not having the slightest idea what was going on.

Of the Socialist Party, only Andrey Babushkin took part in the strike. But luckily, he was forced to break it off to attend our party congress, which took place in Leningrad. Of course, it turned out to be difficult for him to give up the strike, since all the cafes in Leningrad were closed and the food shortage there was even worse than in Moscow. In an effort to have lunch, the hungry and irritable congress delegates tramped from cafes which were "closed for inventory" to restaurants which were "reserved for special functions," to canteens which were simply "closed for lunch."

Meanwhile, the higher echelons of power were hard at work. While the Council deputies fought for Komissarov and Popov and Yeltsin discussed their candidates for the post, Gorbachev took his own decision on the matter: the Moscow GUVD was merged with the regional GUVD and a new boss appointed to head the combined organizations: General Shilov.

Towards the middle of April, events took a tragic turn. On the seventeenth day of the hunger strike, doctors from Memorial [a society dedicated to aiding and commemorating victims of Stalinism] examined the hunger strikers and announced that some of them were in serious danger. Saushkin was beginning to go blind. Bulgakov might even die.

By spring 1991, the first deputies had already died on the job. In Leningrad, a district council deputy had been killed. In Moscow, a City Council deputy, Yury Maksimov, had died in mysterious circumstances. Both had dealt with non-housing-stock real estate. Both cases remain unsolved.

The Council deputies were at last persuaded to break off their hunger strike. The Council again voted by an overwhelming majority to appoint Komissarov head of the Moscow police. He never took up the appointment. According to the Russian authorities, this was due to the opposition of the Communist Minister for USSR Internal Affairs, Boris Pugo. As it later transpired, this explanation was incorrect.

10

PERESTROIKA brought a curious fact to light: in our harsh climate, political life seem to have a relationship with the weather. In the first years of reform, passions seethed in spring and summer, but as soon as the cold weather set in, the situation usually stabilized. It seemed that winter 1990-1991 would be no exception to this rule.

Demonstrations in Moscow not only became a normal occurrence—they attracted fewer and fewer people. The demonstrators were different too. MOI's mobilization machine was still working, but only in fits and starts.

The loss of interest in street rallies attracted particular attention when, on December 9, 1990, only about three thousand people turned up for a Human Rights Day demonstration. By Moscow standards this was a total fiasco.

What a weird demonstration it was!

At Pushkin Square, where the first column gathered, Lev Ubozhko, the self-proclaimed veteran of Russian pluralism, who had already been excluded from three or four parties, spoke for forty minutes on the evils of Marxism. Around him, demonstrators' placards defied description. One called for an end to the annihilation of the people by "KGB micro-letic terror"; another demanded that the orthodox church canonize the innocent Emperor Nicholas II, murdered by the Bolsheviks at the height of the Civil War bloodbath. Some of the slogans were in verse. For example: "The people believe in Yeltsin/ They love him and respect him./ Gorbachev digs him a hole,/ As if he were a little mole." Or: "There was once a happy Rus,/ Where three kopecks could buy you a goose./ But the Communists seized power,/ And the deal on geese went sour."

Soon another crowd, the second column, came up from the Byelorussian station. In the best tradition of totalitarian rallies, they carried many portraits of their leaders: the great warriors against corruption, Gdlyan and Ivanov and, of course, Yeltsin. Waving over the demonstrators' heads was the absolutely traditional slogan: "We support and approve the Yeltsin-Silaev policy!"

The demonstration marched down Tversky, which from habit was still sometimes referred to as Gorky Street. The street was lined with thugs from Pamyat. The demonstrators greeted them joyfully, shouting:

"You are also anticommunists, come and join us!"

The crowd's mood was best conveyed by the words of one of the orators: "We are going to make things really hot for the Communists!" What all this had to do with Human Rights Day is difficult to say.

The orators on Manezh Square kept to their own pet subjects. Ivanov called for the creation of a Russian public prosecutor's office and a Russian army, which, naturally, were to be headed by such stalwart champions from the ranks of the Democrats as Gdlyan, Ivanov, and Colonel Urazhtsev. Most of the speakers talked of the evil deeds perpetrated by the Communists and demanded retribution. Somewhere in the crowd there was a portrait of Andrey Sakharov, but it was lost amidst the numerous portraits of Yeltsin, Gdlyan and Ivanov.

I was also invited to speak as a victim of repression in the Brezhnev era, but on this occasion I didn't mount the tribune. I didn't feel like speaking before this crowd.

For this was no demonstration. It was a panopticon.

After the December rally, political life in the streets of Moscow came to a standstill, but not for long. Just before the New Year, OMON razed the shantytown in front of the Hotel Rossiya. The police were acting on Council's ispolkom instructions, but the following comment was scrawled along the edge of their warrant: "Approved. Stankevich."

Also, on New Year's Eve, deputy Ustinov was beaten up by the police. Ustinov in addition to being a deputy was also on the permanent staff of the KGB. The KGB officers among the deputies were divided among three blocs: the Democrats, the independents, and the Communists. Whereas some handed in their resignation after the election, others kept at their posts, as did Ustinov. As far as anyone can tell, it was because he kept his job he was beaten up—a victim of the traditional antipathy between the police and the KGB.

There was little time to get bored that winter. In January, Gorbachev sent the army to restore order in Lithuania, which had declared its independence. Unarmed people were killed in the street, crushed by tanks. The Western press admitted in some consternation that the marvelous Gorby, whom they had seen as a great defender of democracy, had on this occasion conducted himself somewhat undemocratically. In Moscow, there was a demonstration with anti-Gorbachev and anti-Communist slogans. Protest was essential, and Stankevich, addressing the crowd, announced an emergency session of City Council. But for some reason, he forgot to pass the order on to the *apparat*. And nobody, of course, informed the deputies. Some, out of an old habit from the time of the Popular Front, simply called their friends to tell them. And so, as was only to be expected, there was no quorum. With this, City Council's solidarity with democratic Lithuania came to an end.

On the other hand, on March 28, 1991, when the battle for power between Yeltsin and Gorbachev again was exacerbated, the leaders of DemRossiya organized a truly massive demonstration in the capital, despite the fact that Gorbachev had banned rallies and demonstrations during the spring Congress of People's Deputies of Russia.

The press represented the March demonstration as a decisive action by Muscovites who had taken to the streets to defy the ban. In fact, this was not the case. Gorbachev, in accordance with the rules of the feudal-bureaucratic system which had come into being had, in effect, given City Council the right to free interpretation of his decree. The Council presidium chose to interpret Gorbachev's decree as a ban on all meetings and demonstrations except the pro-Yeltsin demo of March 28. When the action committee of the teachers' union, which was on strike, requested permission to hold its own rally against the Moscow administration's educational policy, it got a refusal: their meeting was banned on the basis of the USSR president's decree. The only exception made was for DemRossiya.

Thus, Gorbachev was caught in a trap of his own making. He could order thousands of soldiers in battle gear onto the streets and cordon off the entrances to the Kremlin, but he could no longer get the city authorities to obey his decree. The demonstration was scrupulously planned and organized directly from the Mossoviet building where, in theory, they should have been drawing up a plan of action for its dispersal. The troops gathered aimlessly in the city center, and neither the soldiers nor the junior officers understood what was going on.

The troops for some reason had been issued camouflage field dress. Even their helmets were covered with camouflage material, which looked absurd in the city. It looked as if the troops were about to be sent off somewhere to fight, but for some reason were being detained in Moscow where they had absolutely nothing to do. The police were also present, OMON and the fire brigade, all getting horribly in each other's way. I walked the length of Tversky, from the Mossoviet to Mayakovsky Square, crossing from one column to another, but I did not find a single officer who could give me a sensible account of what he was doing there.

The atmosphere on the other side was similar. Several hours before the rally, tension reached an all-time high and it seemed as if the country was on the verge of civil war. But the rally came to an end, the crowds dispersed, and nothing happened.

11

ONE CAN keep people in ignorance for a long time. One can manipulate public opinion, making use of a monopoly of the mass media and gagging the discontented, for a very long time. For a long time—but not forever. Sooner or later, the truth comes out.

The longer Gavriil Popov remained in his position as chairman of City Council, the greater the deputies' discontent grew. The electorate saw the city disintegrating before their eyes and blamed the deputies, demanding action from them; the deputies were unable to do anything, since all power was concentrated in the presidium, which simply ignored the Council's existence.

The deputies would probably never have been able to confront their leadership with organized resistance, though, had unexpected help not been forthcoming from the presidium itself.

When the presidium was still being formed, Gavriil Popov had thought it necessary to have someone in the city administration who was capable of coordinating the city's work with that of the district councils. His choice was Nikolay Nikolaevich Gonchar, chairman of the Bauman district council. Although cooperation between the central city administration and its districts was never established, Gonchar hung on to his position as second deputy chairman of City Council. The deputies were used to him chairing Council sittings during Popov's and Stankevich's numerous absences abroad. For a long time Gonchar's political face remained in shadow. He didn't enter into conflict with Popov, nor did he participate in the sharing out of municipal real estate, the setting up of numerous private banks, or the selling off of the city to foreigners. As before, he spent most of his time as before in the district council of which he continued to be chairman.

On several occasions, Gonchar had shown interest in the socialists, although nothing had come of this—until one day in February 1991, when I was stopped on the stairs by a Gonchar aide who said, "Nikolay Nikolaevich wants you to go and see him immediately."

Our meeting took place in Gonchar's office at the Bauman district council. This building, standing right in the center of the city, among nineteenth and even eighteenth century houses, is a typical example of the official architectural style of the Brezhnev period. Walking through old streets, consisting of two-and three-story merchants' houses and nobles' mansions, you suddenly come face to face with a concrete box and immediately realize a seat of power lies before you. At the entrance to the council offices, there used to stand a monstrous sculpture of the usual worker-and-collective-farmgirl couple, but it had been executed in a somewhat untraditional manner. It was an amazing, if not uncommon in the Brezhnev period, combination of socialist realism and modernism, almost in the spirit of Picasso. Instead of holding the huge hammer by its slim, elegantly proportioned handle, the worker, for some reason, seemed to be clinging on to it. The hammer itself appeared to be suspended in the air above the worker's head, and the only reason for him to hold on to it was to stop it from flying away. This sculpture was taken down after the events of August 1992. For all its artistic originality, few mourned its loss.

In a sense, this building, which for a short time became the gathering place of left-wingers, symbolized all that we had hated since childhood in our city. But, later, when we were to come to this building again and again, we ceased to notice the contradiction between the pleasant old Moscow streets and the characterless concrete box in which we held our meetings. We no longer noticed the sculpture by the entrance.

The first time, Gonchar spoke in very abstract terms, but even so, we realized immediately that our positions were the same. We had to try once again to save City Council.

"The Council is not perfect, but it must be saved. To allow the Council to collapse, is to undermine the very principle of representative power. Dictatorship will then be inevitable. What is happening today in Moscow is of the greatest importance for the country as a whole. If we allow the democratic experiment to fail here, it will have fatal consequences for the rest of the country. The main thing is that City Council, for all its imperfections, will prevent violence being done to our city."

This was the gist of what Gonchar said, and we agreed with him. But what were we to do?

We could try again to unite those deputies whose aim was to prevent the collapse of the Council, we could draw up a list of basic demands and attempt to take the initiative. It wasn't long before the deputies who were fed up with the leadership began to gather in Gonchar's office at the Mossoviet, turning it, in effect, into their headquarters.

Rumors of the forthcoming dissolution or "reorganization" of City Council, which had alarmed deputies since the end of the first session, began to acquire substance after Gavriil Popov had won the support of the majority of Muscovites for a referendum on the introduction of the position of mayor in the city. He won outright, since both Popov's supporters—hoping to gain new, unlimited powers for their idol—and his opponents, who saw direct elections as the only way to get rid of the hated city ruler, voted for direct elections for mayor. No one, however, expected Popov to put the results of the referendum to such rapid and effective use: he announced that an election for mayor would be held on June 12, not bothering to wait for either the relevant changes in legislature or the election statutes. For anyone even a little acquainted with the political machinations in the capital, it was clear that under such conditions the election of mayor meant the end of City Council.

And to top it all off, both the Union government and the Russian leadership had drawn up their own projects for administrative reform in Moscow. Although as usual the Union and Russian politicians had nothing but criticism for each other, their proposals were astonishingly similar. Both projects boiled down to the following: limiting the capital's independence, curtailing the powers of the organs of representative democracy, and strengthening the executive power in the office of the mayor. The only difference was that the Union wanted the mayor to be subordinate to itself, while Russia, naturally, wanted the mayor to be answerable to her. This was a death sentence for the district councils, too, in so far as the mayor and whichever power the mayor was subordinate to, from now on would have the right to make changes in the existing administrative and territorial divisions of the city.

Russian parliament deputy Sergei Shakhray, expressing the official opinion of the republic's leadership, wrote a detailed criticism of the Union project in *Kuranty*, condemning it as unconstitutional and antidemocratic. For some reason, he forgot to mention that he had been responsible for drawing up an analogous project for Yeltsin. To the astonishment of the members of the presidium, the deputies not only took note of the danger but began to act with unusual determination to save the Council. An action group, set up by the socialists and greens, with which several rebellious Democrats aligned themselves, demanded that an emergency session be convened. 180 deputies' signatures were gathered on a petition to this effect; draft resolutions were prepared; a temporary statute for the position of mayor of Moscow was drawn up, including a section on election procedures for the post. Moreover, it was stated in the action group's papers that no elections or administrative reform was possible until the relevant amendments had been made to the RSFSR [Russian Socialist Federal Soviet Republic] constitution.

The presidium still didn't understand how serious matters were, however. The city leaders, used to the Council's helplessness, hoped that this time, too, the deputies would "shout their heads off and calm down." It was obvious that the presidium did not intend to convene an emergency session, nor would they have done so, had the deputies not gathered in the Marble Hall themselves on Thursday, April 25.

The deputies demanded a report from those Council deputy chairmen who were present. Stankevich spoke briefly, reiterating what we already knew. He couldn't have spoken in more detail, as he had just returned from America and wasn't *au courant*: only a few minutes before mounting the rostrum, he had tried to find out from me what was afoot.

Gonchar talked at length and very earnestly. The union project, he said, shouldn't be rejected simply because it had been drawn up by the union government. It had to be rejected, though, for a completely different reason: it undermined the principle of representative power. The Russian project was unacceptable for the same reason. He also said that, while changing the slogans, the new leaders of Russia had retained the principle of like-mindedness. As in Stalin's time, he said, the concentration camp regulation "a step out of line to the left or right will be regarded as an attempt to escape, and the guard will shoot without warning," was still in force in our society.

There was no quorum and therefore the emergency session could not be convened, but more than half the members of the Council were present. We decided to hold the emergency session on Monday, and the presidium was entrusted with making the necessary arrangements. Still not understanding what was going on, Aleksandr Sokolov, speaking on behalf of the leadership, appealed to the rebellious deputies to calm down and disperse since, he said, they were powerless to decide anything. Only the presidium could pass resolutions. This didn't work. Sokolov didn't realize that a turning point had been reached: the deputies had now mastered the basics of political warfare.

At that moment, however, there was a lot we didn't know. We didn't know, for example, that while the deputies were discussing the mayoralty issue, the chief candidate for this post, Gavriil Popov, had already drafted the election statutes. The day after the meeting in the Marble Hall, this draft lay on Yeltsin's desk. Within one more day, it had "in the main been approved" by the presidium of the Russian Supreme Soviet. While the debate was underway in the Council, the still-unelected mayor Popov and the still-unelected president Yeltsin had already reached agreement on the capital's future.

The regulations Popov had drawn up were, in its way, unique. To register a candidate 72,000 signatures had to be collected—that is to say, 1 percent of the total number of voters in the capital. Signatures were not to be gathered in the street, at the workplace, or in the home. No signatures at all, in fact, were to be gathered. "The voter, wishing to support a candidate for mayor of Moscow," the document read, "will be given a stamped tear-off coupon at his local polling station on which will be indicated the surname, Christian names, patronymic, date of birth, and passport details of the said voter. A tick, denoting that a coupon has been issued, will be entered in the voters' list. The voter himself will write, on the reverse side of the coupon, the surname of the candidate he supports. The completed coupons will be submitted to the electoral commission and against the voter's surname the name of the candidate to whom he gave his support will be recorded in ink." To top everything off, it was stated in the draft statutes that "a voter may give his support to no more than one candidate." There was no question, then, of a secret ballot.

This procedure was so reminiscent of that for obtaining coupons for vodka and tobacco, introduced a few months before by the same Moscow leadership, that in the Russian Supreme Soviet they immediately called it the coupon system. Even if Popov's signature hadn't been at the bottom of the document, it would have been recognizable as his work.

The point of this ploy was clear. Apart from the Communist Party and DemRossiya no other organization in the capital would be able to round up 72,000 people willing to go to the polling stations and do what was required. Especially since, according to Popov's plan, the whole operation had to be completed within twenty days. There was only one thing, incidentally, that he had overlooked: there was no stamp at the polling stations, so the coupons couldn't be officially endorsed.

If to be nominated via Popov's statute was difficult, to be elected turned out to be easy. One of the paragraphs of his draft began with the following sentence: "If in the voting-paper, only one candidate is entered..." It is not difficult to guess this candidate's name.

The candidate for mayor had thought of almost everything—except, perhaps, one thing. On the evening of the same day, a copy of the draft, together with an accompanying letter from Popov, written on his letterhead and bearing his personal signature, lay on my desk. The person who delivered the document repeated several times that he had no idea where it had come from or who had passed it on. I could, perhaps, have ventured a guess, but decided to keep my suppositions to myself: the important thing was that the document was now in my hands.

Both sides prepared for the emergency session as for a decisive battle. The opposition met in Gonchar's office, to which any deputy or Council staff member had free access. Gonchar himself came and went, but didn't take part in the work of the organizing committee for the session. The Council presidium met behind closed doors. They forgot to invite Gonchar: he was considered unreliable. Deputies, contrary to normal procedure, were not admitted. When I, oblivious to the secrecy, tried to enter Stankevich's room with some papers, I was unexpectedly barred by Sokolov, who had the following pointless, although quite understandable, question:

"What the hell do you think you're doing?"

I did not have the slightest desire to attend this meeting. My knowledge of the Bible was enough to know that it was better not to walk in the "counsel of the ungodly."

The city leaders took other precautions. In particular, they began to watch Gonchar, and they did this quite openly. Either Vasily Shakhnovsky or someone else from Stankevich and Popov's inner circle was always hanging around him, listening to his conversations, taking note of whom he spoke to. During one of my talks with Gonchar, Shakhnovsky simply walked into his office and, without asking for permission, sat down behind me. Since during the perestroika years I had got out of the habit of being openly shadowed, I broke off my conversation and, having bid the deputy chairman of the Council goodbye, I left the room, leaving him alone with Popov's trusted agent. After I had gone, Gonchar was forced to listen to what amounted, in effect, to an ultimatum.

"Your speech," Shakhnovsky said, "was the speech of a socialist. That's a challenge."

It was indeed a challenge, a challenge to blind subordination, to the tradition of the mutual protection racket, to incompetence and corruption.

"It may be that the City Council is useless," Gonchar had said. "But this is a reflection of the city. Its failings are the failings of society. It may be ineffective, but it will never pass a resolution which is unacceptable to the majority of our citizens. If City Council goes, our citizens' last defense will be gone."

On the morning of Monday April 29, the deputies began to gather for the emergency session.

The Marble Hall buzzed like a stirred-up beehive. There was no problem reaching a quorum. The deputies arrived for the sitting on time.

On the stage, places had been prepared for Gavriil Popov and Sergei Stankevich as well as for Frolov, Zheludkov, and Aleksandr Popov, who were to speak on behalf of the organizing committee of the session. The proceedings began with an attempt by Stankevich to prevent deputy Shalnov, a member of the Moscow Left-Wingers whom the organizing committee had requested to inform the Council of the session's business, from speaking. For about half an hour before the official opening of the session, Stankevich squabbled with the floor and the organizing committee, but finally the session was opened and the floor given not to Shalnov, but to Popov. This city father had nothing important to tell us. The presidium's trump card was the speech given by Sergei Shakhray, who had been specially summoned to the Mossoviet for this purpose.

Shakhray had an unenviable task. Someone asked whether

the proposed innovations contravened the constitution of the RSFSR. This lawyer, one of Yeltsin's men, answered that as far as the constitution was concerned one might simply make an exception, but that this didn't in any way represent an infringement of the country's basic law. Andrey Babushkin wanted to know whether the theft of deputy Shakhray's personal car might not constitute an exceptional circumstance, in no way infringing the general principles of the criminal code.

Fending off attacks of this sort, Shakhray, speaking on behalf of the Russian leadership, mentioned Gavriil Popov's letter, not knowing that the presidium had assured us that they had not sent any documents to the Russian parliament. He used the words "coupon system," among others.

By this time, several copies of Popov's letter were already circulating around the hall. In one deputy's hands, I even saw the full text of Popov's celebrated proposal for statutes for the election of mayor (I was afterwards to learn that my colleague did not have the slightest idea of the importance of this document).

When my turn came to speak, I spent my allotted three minutes simply quoting the most striking parts of the Popov document. The impact of this surpassed all my expectations. Popov lost his temper. Forgetting protocol, he tried to stop me.

"Stop talking garbage," he shouted.

And it was indeed garbage. But its author sat in the presidium. I had showed the floor the document, which bore Popov's signature.

"If this text isn't genuine, you have the right to say so. But it bears your signature."

He said nothing.

"Gavriil Kharitonovich," I continued, "we all know your weakness for coupons, vouchers, and identity cards, but coupons for democracy is going too far!"

The floor guffawed.

Before the break, Popov was offered the floor to reply, but he refused. For the rest of the day, Gavriil Kharitonovich remained silent. All the resolutions drawn up by the organizing committee of the session were adopted without major alterations. The deputies voted for a new proposal for statutes for the position of mayor and for fairly democratic procedures for the registration of candidates. 10,000 signatures were enough, and they could be gathered anywhere: in the metro, on the street, on the shopfloor. The elections could not be held until the relevant amendments had been made to the laws and the constitution. The session completed its work in one day, showing that even City Council deputies were capable of working effectively when not hindered by the presidium.

Gavriil Kharitonovich is not the sort of person who takes kindly to defeat. The next day, not one of the leading Moscow newspapers bothered to inform its readers of the results of the session. When members of the organizing committee turned up at state television, they were told that the chairman of City Council himself would acquaint Muscovites with the outcome of the session.

What took place that evening at state television even took Muscovites, who were used to everything, by surprise. First to appear on the air was a representative of the Moscow group, Shantsev, who announced that the session had taken place thanks to the constant concern of Moscow Communists for democracy in the city. The so-called minor factions who had also participated in the organization of the session were also mentioned in passing, although Shantsev didn't say what we had done. Shantsev was followed by deputy Krugovykh, speaking on behalf of the independents, who declared that everything that had occurred was due to the efforts of his group. Neither found it necessary to inform viewers of the content of the adopted resolutions. Muscovites were left knowing neither whom they should thank nor what to thank for.

Immediately after Krugovykh, Gavriil Popov appeared on the screen smiling benignly. Contradicting Shantsev, the city father explained that the Moscow Democrats had won yet another victory: they had condemned the antidemocratic projects of the union government and supported the wise projects of the Russian parliament. Gavriil Kharitonovich gave an especially detailed and inspired account of the new democratic procedures for the registration of candidates for mayor. Now, at last, viewers understood that another Communist plot had been foiled and that thanks for this were due, as always, to their leader Gavriil Kharitonovich.

But it wasn't long before this version of events, too, was placed in doubt. When the hockey match, which had distracted viewers from their political passions, came to an end, thousands of viewers returned again to the Moscow channel. They saw Aleksandr Popov and Anatoly Zheludkov on the screen, and the announcer told them that an unprecedented incident had taken place: the deputies had demanded to be allowed on the air. Central television had been "taken by storm." Numerous telephone calls, prolonged negotiations, pleas, and demands had eventually brought results. The organizing committee of the emergency session was now given the opportunity to speak.

This time, Muscovites were told that the presidium hadn't helped at all in getting the session convened, and that, "unfortunately," as Aleksandr put it, Gavriil Popov had misinformed viewers. City Council had not supported the Russian parliament, as they had been told but, on the contrary, had entered into conflict with it.

It was not easy to make sense out of all this. More likely than not, most viewers decided that what had taken place was simply beyond comprehension. But even so, many in the city began to suspect that Gavriil Kharitonovich might not be speaking the truth. The more time passed, the stronger this suspicion grew.

12

THE APPROACHING mayoral elections caused the city fathers to take their popularity very seriously. Popov's minions discussed various projects for boosting his image; they decided on a dip through a hole in the ice. Muscovites were about to celebrate Fitness Day, and Popov's aides requested him to take part. Photographers were invited. Popov wavered until he was reminded that George Bush thought nothing of jogging in his shorts in the presence of TV journalists. Hearing of his boss's decision, Luzhkov, without a moment's hesitation, also agreed to take a plunge through the ice.

This public relations exercise was very well planned, except for the fact that the sportive, slim figure of the American president made for a much prettier photograph than did the corpulent, sagging bodies of the Moscow leaders. But, as invariably happens, the less attractive aspects of the events were forgotten. Popov jumped through the hole in the ice and immediately hopped out again. Luzhkov, for appearances' sake, wallowed about for several minutes. The next day, a picture of our leaders climbing out of the icy water appeared on the sports page of *Moskovsky Komsomolets*. The city's leaders took to the ceremony so much that there was a repeat performance the following year.

In fact, the election depended on neither a candidate's

popularity nor even his platform. The opposition lacked viable candidates.

Everyone in Gavriil Popov's camp was convinced that he would win. Neither the numerous scandals affecting the city leadership, nor the collapse of the city's economy, nor even the failure of various publicity stunts caused his supporters any anxiety. They knew that Yeltsin and the Russian government were on their side.

About a week after the City Council's emergency session, the presidium of the Russian Supreme Soviet published its own regulations for elections for mayor of Moscow. The City Council resolutions were simply ignored; the Russian regulations were based on the same proposals of Gavriil Popov that had aroused such a scandal at the session. True, the more absurd statutes, such as the coupons, had been wisely removed, and the "starting price" had been lowered to 35,000 signatures—but in effect the document remained largely unchanged.

It was like bartering in the marketplace. Having encountered opposition from the deputies, the Russian leaders had given us "half price," while at the same time making it understood that 35,000 was their final offer.

Contenders were given less than a month for the collection of signatures and the election campaign. To run for president of Russia, a candidate was required to collect no more than 100,000 signatures. It followed from the new statutes that—in proportion to number of voters—it was four times harder to be nominated for mayor of Moscow. Deputies joked ruefully that if Yeltsin thought 35 percent of the population of Russia lived in Moscow, he should give us 35 percent of the budget.

The Russian leaders' aim was obvious: to prevent the democratic opposition from taking part in the elections, and to make the nomination of independent candidates impossible. All posts and appointments were to be contended for by only Dem-Rossiya representatives or Communist Party functionaries. Another thing was clear: the leaders of DemRossiya were no longer confident they would win free elections in Moscow. There was only one way they could strengthen their position: by toppling democracy. For the time being, the Communist Party would be the only opposition. This would make it possible, on the one hand, to appeal for constant struggle against the "Red Terror," to demand that the democrats "consolidate their ranks," and to accuse all dissenters of playing into the hands of the Communists; on the other hand, it would guarantee success to DemRossiya's leaders since the CPSU represented no real threat to them. Enjoying the support of only 10 percent of the voters, torn apart by internal strife, having no platform or strategy, and absolutely discredited, the Communist Party was simply incapable of playing a serious role in the capital's political life after 1990.

Street demonstrations were to be the monopoly of Dem-Rossiya. The first case of this was the ban on the teachers' rally in March. At the time, the authorities hid behind Gorbachev's decree. By April, the decree was no longer in force but the practice of bans continued. Following their ban of the teachers' rally, the City Council ispolkom refused to give a student group permission for a rally. The students were trying to win themselves compensation to make up for the rise in cost of living. Their organizing committee agreed to observe the ban, but just to be on the safe side, the city authorities called out a division of OMON onto Soviet Square and instructed them not to allow any "unsanctioned rallies."

The pacification of *Moskovsky Komsomolets* had given Popov and Luzhkov carte blanche to do as they liked. There was no need to worry particularly about the City Council deputies. Possessing neither access to the mass media nor the right to street protests, any opposition on the Council was doomed to impotence. But for all that the discontent with Popov's politics on the Council grew with each hour—let alone day—that passed.

Aware of the growing tension, Gavriil Kharitonovich decided to strike the pose of injured party and explain to the people that all his previous failures had been due not to his own irresponsibility or incompetence, but to sabotage by the evil deputies. This was particularly important since no one believed in Communist sabotage anymore, and therefore a new scapegoat had to be found. It wasn't difficult to find a pretext for accusing City Council of ingratitude. As the elections for mayor approached, Gavriil Kharitonovich and his supporters demanded that City Council nominate him for mayor and, at the same time, Yeltsin for president.

One has to hand it to the deputies. Over the past year they had become sufficiently conversant with the ABC's of state law to realize that the representative branch simply could not and should not nominate candidates for election to the executive branch. It would be amusing to see, for instance, how U.S. democracy would work if a candidate for president were to be nominated by Congress, and the political parties told to compete with this official candidate according to rules of the latter's making. But this was just what Gavriil Popov and those Democrats loyal to him were trying to engineer. Popov's supporters, moreover, demanded that the vote be by name so that they would know which of the deputies had supported the nomination and which hadn't.

City Council of course refused to nominate Yeltsin and Popov. This was just what Popov had been waiting for. The very next day, indignant articles appeared in the press, full of accusations against the deputies who had shown themselves to be so ungrateful and had even turned out to be traitors. For some reason, it was not Gavriil Popov who should be grateful to the deputies for having elected him chairman of City Council (which the majority now deeply regretted), but the deputies themselves who should be grateful to their chairman for having bothered to put up with them for a whole year. One article even stated that if it had not been for the support of Popov and Yeltsin, none of the Democrats would have been elected to City Council. (If that had happened, one can't help wondering whom Popov would have worked with and who would have elected him chairman.)

Yeltsin's supporters read out the lists of "traitors" at rallies. On May 21, 1991 a large crowd of DemRossiya supporters gathered in front of the Mossoviet. They were there, they said, to protest the central government's policies in Armenia. Of

Armenia, though, there was no mention; instead, Gavriil Popov addressed the crowd from the balcony of the Mossoviet and demanded the immediate dissolution of the Council since the deputies had "betrayed" him.

Things were heating up on the Council itself. Speaking at the session, Kondratov and Khramov reminded their listeners that "free elections" had paved the way for fascism in Germany. Even if the June elections turned out to be relatively free, there would be no guarantee that the victors would take minority rights and citizens' opinions into account. The new leaders wanted elections at this moment not in order to strengthen democracy, but in order to get a mandate to do as they liked: to get rid of the laws and democratic representative organs they thought were unnecessary obstacles to the implementation of the "firmly expressed popular will."

When his turn came, Vladimir Bokser, the leader of Dem-Rossiya, didn't mince words. At a meeting of the movement's supporters, he said that anyone at that moment not supporting Gavriil Popov and Boris Yeltsin was "a political corpse." The session heard about this and a new scandal broke out.

Walking calmly up to a mike, Yury Khramov stood in the middle of the keyed-up hall and reminded his fellow deputies that he had been against a name vote, but now he was for it, "so that people would know who was responsible for bringing the new Stalins and Schicklgrubers to power." As Khramov was making his way back to his seat, deputy Chernyak threw himself at him with an angry shout and tried to hit him in the face. Khramov, an experienced karate expert, deflected the blow. The hall erupted into disorder. The next day, the press reported that the socialist deputy had made an insulting comment about Popov, which had rightly aroused the anger of the democratic deputies. *Kommersant* ("The Businessman") stated gleefully that the socialist had been "punched in the face." Khramov's popularity soared.

Since the leftist opposition had no hope of getting on television and the press was openly hostile, its main vehicle for appealing to citizens was the independent radio station Ekho Moskvy. This radio station, located in an attractive (though not a bit suited for broadcasting) old building literally a stone's throw from the Kremlin, was one of the few remaining holdouts of independent journalism. The political views of its staff could hardly have been described as left-wing or radical, but they tried to speak the truth and to inform their listeners of the facts without being bothered about whose advantage these facts bolstered. Here, not only those in power and the Communists, but even the socialists were allowed on the air. It wasn't long before Ekho Moskvy came under fire. *Nezavisimaya Gazeta* ("The Independent Newspaper") which, despite its title, had been set up by City Council and firmly supported the political line of DemRossiya, published a sharply-worded article against Ekho Moskvy. The ruling circles' attitude toward the radio station took a sharp turn for the worse, but its journalists continued to do their job.

Thanks to this radio station, Vladimir Kondratov, Aleksandr Popov, and I managed to appear on the air. The Ekho Moskvy journalists didn't play games with their studio guests; they demanded clear, unambiguous answers that would convince a skeptical audience.

To the surprise of the socialists, the weekly *Kommersant* began publishing detailed and objective reports on what was happening in the city and at the Mossoviet. This strange newspaper, in which business information was interspersed with malicious jokes, was famous for its ironic headlines which, before long, all the Moscow papers began to imitate. At first, *Kommersant*, like the rest of the press, was inclined to sing the praises of the free market and laud Russian business, but as Communism increasingly became a propagandist bogey, the *Kommersant* journalists began to write in a different vein. It soon became clear that the policies of the "liberal" Russian bureaucracy was even more harmful for small and average-size businesses than those of the old Communist regime. In addition, *Kommersant* didn't suffer fools and adored scandals—and in the corridors of the White and Red Houses there were more than enough of both. "A typical case of the radicalization of the petty bourgeoisie," said one of my Western sociologist friends.

Kommersant was not shy about offending Gavriil Popov and writing the truth about Yeltsin. It was thanks to Ekho Moskvy and *Kommersant*, both of which refused to allow the opposition to be completely silenced, that the city learned at least something about what was happening at the Mossoviet. And since central television couldn't afford to completely ignore this, we sometimes managed to force our way onto TV, too.

The TV interviews were often bizarre.

"You talk about straight government," said the interviewer in disbelief, having listened to Kondratov's description of the corruption on the Council. "Is such a thing possible? Isn't that like talking about fried ice? Give us some examples!"

"President Allende," said Kondratov.

"And some others."

"Franklin Delano Roosevelt."

The next day, one of the deputies from the Gagarin district council shouted at Kondratov: "We'll shoot you from the same machine gun as Allende!" This didn't sound like a joke.

In the meantime, Gavriil Popov was conducting his election campaign in a strange fashion. Having taken offense at the deputies, he pretended for a while that he didn't want to put himself forward for nomination at all. In the press and on the radio and TV, "public opinion" humbly begged an obdurate Gavriil Kharitonovich to change his mind. Well, perhaps he would put himself forward after all, he finally said, but only if afterwards he was given emergency powers.

This reminded one of the opening scenes of Pushkin's *Boris Godunov*, in which the boyars lead the completely muddled and confused crowd to beg Boris to accept the throne, knowing full well what the result would be. As an educated man, perhaps Gavriil Kharitonovich couldn't resist acting out this small production in the classical vein.

Everything was going according to plan and triumph was almost within his grasp when things were marred by the appearance of a rival. Tatyana Koryagina, economist and Russian Republic parliament deputy, announced her intention of running for mayor of Moscow.

Koryagina was nominated by the Moscow section of the Socialist Party, which in itself was sensational. Koryagina had come to public attention as a supporter of radical market reform. She had been one of the first people in the country to demand the legalization of private property, after which she had joined forces with the famous investigators Gdlyan and Ivanov in exposing corruption in the upper echelons of power. DemRossiya had intended to make her minister of defense. But then a rupture occurred.

Having gone most of the way with DemRossiya, Koryagina suddenly realized that the leaders of this movement were not concerned, as they claimed to be, about the people's well-being, and nor could they care less about democracy. Although they condemned corruption, they were not entirely innocent in this respect—in many cases, they were much worse offenders than those against whom they fulminated.

Her disappointment in the DemRossiya leaders was accompanied by a more precise reformulation of her political position. Now, Koryagina emphasized that while she supported the legalization of private property, she had never been a supporter of rapid and large-scale privatization; that the mafia and the bureaucracy were making use of the slogans of the free market to conceal their real goal, which was to lay hands on state property; and that the country needed a socially-oriented market economy, not experiments in the spirit of misunderstood neoliberalism.

When we heard that Koryagina was seriously thinking of running for mayor, Anatoly Baranov and I went to visit her in the hospital where she happened to be at the time. In spite of her health problems, Koryagina decided to run for deputy mayor. The Socialist Party nominated Aleksandr Popov. Koryagina's nomination aroused alarm in the official camp. Countermeasures were taken immediately. An interview with Koryagina, due to be published in *Moskovsky Komsomolets*, was spiked. Gdlyan and Ivanov, evidently not without the influence of other DemRossiya politicians, refused to support her. Infighting began among their supporters. In Zelenograd, where

Koryagina had been nominated as a deputy to the Russian parliament, people were frightened to collect signatures in support of her candidacy for mayor since the recalcitrant economist had already been branded a turncoat.

Virtually the entire job of signature collecting fell to the small Moscow section of the Socialist Party. We received very little help even from the greens, not to mention the other left-wing groups which preferred to continue their theoretical discussions of the benefits or evils of a market economy.

To collect 35,000 signatures under such conditions was impossible. But the attempt to collect them gave us a better feel for the mood in the city. To our surprise, there had been a big change. While the majority of the workers were, as before, hostile towards those in power, the engineers and students had been brainwashed by the Gavriilopopists.

We had truly underestimated the power of propaganda. The most astonishing thing for us was that the worse the situation got, the more people who hadn't benefited from the new administration—and who had even suffered at its hands—were prone to swallow the declarations of the ruling elite. Gavriil Popov and Sergei Stankevich appeared on TV nearly every Tuesday, explaining that all the city's problems were either due to the machinations of enemies or had been inherited from the Communist administration. The appeal for strong government, the promise to carry out reforms with an iron hand, constant references to the incompetence of the deputies—all this found support with the majority of the people.

Homo Sovieticus, thanks to decades of Communist power, turned out to be astonishingly naive and unprepared for the new dangers. Having ceased to believe the Communist slogans, this creature was ready to accept uncritically any blatant lie, as long as it wasn't Communist demagogy.

In their year in power, the City Council leaders had set up a powerful propaganda machine which included the Council mouthpiece *Kuranty*, and the magazines *Stolitsa* and *Moya Moskva* ("My Moscow"). All these papers were fully dependent on the administration both organizationally and financially;

their editors in chief were appointed from among the deputies belonging to the ruling majority. The administration carried out its propaganda through *Nezavisimaya Gazeta* too.

The Russian administration in turn established its own propaganda apparatus, including Russian television and radio, *Rossiyskaya Gazeta* ("The Russian Newspaper"), and other papers. In terms of its scale, this processing of public opinion was equal to the old propaganda efforts of the CPSU. In terms of impact, as we were soon to discover, it surpassed them. Most of the journalists came from the old Party press, and they put existing propaganda methods to excellent use in the service of their new masters.

It was the Communist leadership who set up between 1986 and 1988 what was later to become known as the "democratic press." Yegor Yakovlev, Vitaly Korotich, Pavel Guzev, and the other editors of the opposition press had been appointed by decision of the CPSU Central Committee, and they constantly had to do the rounds of the highest echelons of power to get approval for the pieces they published. Not one truly independent paper had really gotten on its feet in recent years. The administration, first Communist, then Democratic, kept strict control over paper—the prices for which rose astronomically—and distribution outlets. Later on, government subsidies of the press were to become a decisive factor for control. The small *samizdat* newspapers and magazines either shut down or eked out a miserable existence on the fringe of public life. The editorial offices of the main papers were subject to purges—what happened to *Moskovsky Komsomolets* was no exception. Due to the disorder in newspaper offices and the incompetence of editors in chief, journalists sometimes managed to get truthful articles published—now in one paper, now in another. But this was obviously insufficient to beat the powerful propaganda machine which the joint efforts of the CPSU and DemRossiya had built up.

Totalitarian propaganda methods guaranteed the success of the Yeltsin and Popov campaigns. This time, in contrast to 1990, there were neither leaflets setting forth programs nor even short texts saying how the new leaders intended to work for the good of the country and the capital. There weren't even any political slogans. Instead, there were just colorful posters bearing portraits of the leaders and such high-sounding phrases as "Russia's prosperity, Moscow's well-being" or "Moscow's Future is In Reliable Hands!" Portraits of Yeltsin were put up around town, bearing the following caption: "I'm voting for Popov and Luzhkov."

Such methods had also been used in the 1990 campaign, but the main emphasis had been on more weighty arguments. Now, the rulers of Moscow and Russia addressed appeals to their subjects which came close to being commands. The new state flag of Russia, which doubled up as the DemRossiya flag, was hung out everywhere. Colorful portraits of Yeltsin were put up all over the place. Around the statue of Yury Dolgoruky, the founder of Moscow, Yeltsinists set up an open-air, 24-hour agitation center. About a dozen identical portraits of the leader were plastered on the base of the statue, so that Yeltsin looked at us from all directions. There were postcards with his portrait on one side and a quote from him on the other. As usual in such cases, the utterances of the people's leader were utter banalities: "We'll do everything to make the Russian family strong and prosperous. A happy home means a happy state!"

Somewhat less often, one came across portraits of Colonel Rutskoy, Yeltsin's candidate for vice president. With other Moscow Popular Front activists, I had come across Rutskoy back in 1989 at the elections for USSR people's deputies. In those days, this air force pilot and hero of the war in Afghanistan had been a candidate for the Russian nationalists. The Pamyat was always prominent at his rallies. All the Democrats in the Kuntsev district, where these skirmishes took place, had joined in order to prevent Rutskoy's election. This time around, the very same Democrats were fighting no less cordially in order to get the heroic colonel made vice president of Russia.

Before the elections, DemRossiya activists received campaign instructions compiled by anonymous experts. This remarkably frank document recommended that leaflets and other publicity material be published in the press, for this "would economize on both the time and money spent on posting up fliers, calling labor collectives, and so on." An example to emulate was the publication of a DemRossiya leaflet in the Moscow newspaper *Kuranty*. These fliers could then be cut out of the papers and posted.

Kuranty, financed by the taxpayers, theoretically should have maintained neutrality during the campaign, making its pages available to all political groups in equal measure. But the DemRossiya leaders had come up with one for the books: instead of spending time and money on publishing their own newspapers, they could simply get the city's inhabitants to pay for having their own brains washed!

According to the DemRossiya propaganda experts, it was essential for "letters from the workers" to be published in the press explaining why "this time they had decided quite definitely to vote for B. N. Yeltsin." The letters should be from "an elderly Communist, a serviceman, and a mullah of the Muslim faith from Tartarstan." As was to be expected, it wasn't long before letters answering to this description appeared in the papers.

It was likewise recommended that the results of opinion polls be published—but not all of them. "If these results indicate an obvious majority for B. N. Yeltsin and his candidate for vice president, their publication may attract to our side all those who are still wavering. The so-called line effect comes into operation: seeing a line, a man develops a wish to buy something which, if it had not been for the line, he wouldn't have even noticed." In this case, the commodities which had to be sold at any price were Yeltsin, Rutskoy, Popov, and Luzhkov. "Seeing how the majority support B. N. Yeltsin, the person still in doubt may, 'like everyone else,' give his vote to the candidate enjoying nationwide trust."

As was to be expected, the papers began one after another to publish fantastic results, which had ostensibly been obtained from opinion polls. All bore witness to an overwhelming lead of Gavriil Popov. There was even a report in *Moskovsky Kom-*

somolets that less than 1 percent of Muscovites were going to vote for Koryagina. However, a poll engaged by the City Council deputies indicated something quite different. Koryagina held a steady second place, Popov appeared to be getting between 29 and 37 percent of the voters, while 40 percent were not decided. Yeltsin was supported by just over half the Muscovites, which was certainly not sufficient to talk about nationwide trust.

If the Yeltsinists waged a confident and aggressive campaign, the helpless Communist candidates gave little sign of life. The CPSU had been unable to nominate a single candidate. Several Communists ran for mayor at the same time, and the party gorkom supported them all! Communists ran for president and vice president of Russia on virtually all the lists, though; after all, even Rutskoy who was running with Yeltsin was a member of the Communist Party.

No matter what the CPSU members did, they were not excluded from the party. They were not required to adhere to its rules and program. This could only mean one of two things: either the CPSU had ceased to exist as a political organization, or it hadn't yet come into existence.

One of the more colorful candidates for mayor of Moscow was Mrs. Rodionova, chairperson of the Radost ("Joy") cooperative. Rodionova's platform called for free urban transport and the deportation of all people with AIDS to a "comfortable satellite town where they'd be under the observation of specialists." Unlike us, Rodionova didn't encounter any serious problems collecting signatures: she paid her collectors a rouble a piece, thirty-five rubles for a full list. For some 40,000 rubles, she managed to collect the requisite number of signatures. The majority of these signatures, of course, turned out to be fakes. There was no time to check them—the collectors were paid immediately in cash. Someone had the bright idea of simply copying out the entries in the Union of Writers' telephone directory. And so it transpired that all the writers in Moscow— slavophiles and Westerners, Communists and liberals, Socialists and fascists—had cordially nominated Rodionova as their candidate. Since directories in our country are not published every year, there turned out to be quite a few corpses among Rodionova's supporters, too.

Rodionova's lists were rejected by the commission, but she was reinstated as a candidate by the city court, which ruled that there was insufficient evidence to refuse her the right to register.

Koryagina managed to collect about 11,600 signatures. This was sufficient according to the City Council statutes, but the commission decreed that candidates should be guided exclusively by the statutes drawn up by Gavriil Popov for the presidium of the Supreme Soviet of Russia. Despite the repeated protests of City Council deputies and even a special Council resolution, the elections were conducted according to the absurd Russian rules.

13

THE OUTCOME had been decided in advance; there was virtually no battle. Several days before the election, Gavriil Popov published his platform in *Nezavisimaya Gazeta*. Few of the city's inhabitants read this unexpectedly extensive document, with its borrowed title "The City for its Citizens," right through. Plagiarism of other people's ideas and formulas had always been one of Gavriil Kharitonovich's strong points— when, at the beginning of the perestroika era, Popov had quoted whole paragraphs from Ota Sik and other Eastern European "revisionists" without mentioning sources, his colleagues had just shrugged their shoulders. A few had even been inclined to regard it as heroic: to mention Sik at the time after all had been risky, and by not doing so Popov had been introducing these ideas into academic circulation.

In the course of his career, Popov had in this way "introduced into academic circulation" the ideas of many American management theoreticians and economists. This time around, luckily for us, Popov's borrowings from the platform of the Moscow socialists were limited to the above-quoted title. The rest of his program boiled down to a wordy and self-contradictory discussion on the theme of privatization—or, as the candidate for mayor preferred to put it, de-state-ization. It was proposed to "de-state-ize" all spheres of economic activity—housing, com-

merce, consumer services, industry, the health system, education, and culture.

Gavriil Kharitonovich did not promise to privatize state
power. But in effect this was already being done. When, after
prolonged efforts, Vladimir Kondratov, Anatoly Baranov, and I
managed at the beginning of June to get onto Moscow television
to talk about the deals that had been closed in the city, the
camera operators and news anchors were stunned. It was then
that many Muscovites heard for the first time about the amazing
project for the reconstruction of Gagarin Square. This huge
square, together with adjacent buildings (sixty-six hectares in
all), had been rented out to a joint enterprise KNIT-Kaluga Gate
(set up by the French firm Compagnie Generale De Batiments
et Constructions and the joint-stock company SARI) for the
modest sum of ten dollars a year for ninety-nine years (despite
the fact existing laws prohibited rents for terms of over fifty
years). On this site, French companies were to build a center for
new industries and technologies. They'd already built a similar
center in Paris and—as was later to come to light—there, too,
the project was accompanied by dubious machinations which
attracted the attention of the prosecutor's office. Popov and
Luzhkov went on energetically pushing the Moscow deal even
after it was widely known that several of the participants were
under investigation in Paris.

The Gagarin Square deal offered generous tax concessions,
numerous sanctions against the Soviet side should it not fulfill
its obligations, and virtually total freedom to the French companies to act as they pleased. The Soviet participants were given
the right not to enter their profits in the city's budget, but to
transfer them instead to "organizations linked corporatively to
themselves." And thus not only the French, but their Moscow
partners as well (who came mainly from the city administration)
were able to pocket large sums.

Blocks of apartments in the Gagarin Square area came under
threat of demolition. When later on, after the elections, residents began hearing rumors that the French were going to have
them evicted, Popov made a public statement with the aim of

calming the locals down: "Joint enterprises can't evict anyone. The mayor's office will look into the matter, and it, naturally, will do the evicting."

It proved impossible to put an end to the Gagarin Square scandal. Despite all the efforts of the city leaders, it continued to grow, until they finally managed to hush it up before the elections. And that scandal was only the tip of the iceberg. Like mushrooms after a shower, strange companies popped up all over the place, engaged either in selling off the city or in pumping municipal funds into the pockets of new entrepreneurs. Take for example the joint-stock company Orgkomitet, whose chairman was Luzhkov. This company had virtually a complete monopoly on the real estate business in Moscow.

In America, political careers have been destroyed for less. But here, things are different. The people we publicly accused of corruption didn't bother to object or to refute the accusations. They didn't take us to court. They didn't argue with us. They simply laughed at our appeals for clean government and calmly went on as before. When *Kommersant* journalists took up the matter with the official representatives of those who were implicated in the Gagarin Square scandal, they were told without the slightest hesitation that their information was correct, but that the deal was very profitable for the city since it would attract foreign capital. Worst of all, the city's inhabitants appeared to accept this.

I kept hearing: "Yes, they probably are stealing, but then here everyone steals!" Or: "Power corrupts—doing anything in an honest way is impossible."

Under Brezhnev there was probably no less corruption but people kept it hidden. The absence of freedom of speech generally made it impossible to expose bureaucrats caught stealing, but on those rare occasions when scandalous facts did come out in the open, the guilty parties were punished, as a rule, by being transferred to less prominent posts. At the beginning of the 1980s, after all, even members of the Brezhnev family got in trouble!

In the era of glasnost, particularly after DemRossiya's victory, the atmosphere changed. Even facts which had been indisputably proved didn't change anything and didn't mean anything. Millions of people reacted to the reports of huge bribes and abuses of public office with envy, not anger. Thieving, betrayal, deceit, and extortion became methods worthy of respect—so long as they were crowned with success.

We were living in strange times. The boom in pornography was accompanied by active efforts to strengthen the church. The introduction of computers coincided with mass enthusiasm for astrology and black magic. The selling off of our country went hand in hand with slogans proclaiming its sovereignty. Politicians speaking openly about the benefits of unemployment were regarded as the main protectors of workers' interests. And fascism gained strength—to the applause of the liberal intelligentsia who saw it as the only viable form of democracy.

14

WE HAVE believed too long in the magic of words. Thus changes in the power structure arouse less interest than changes in slogans. The renaming of cities, streets, and public offices is taken as proof of the triumph of democracy—especially if the new names are borrowed from the age of the absolute monarchy.

In June 1991 the Chairman of the Moscow City Council became known as the mayor of the city, while the leader of the Council ispolkom acquired the impressive-sounding title of Deputy Mayor and Premier of the Government of Moscow. Instead of heads of section there were now ministers of city government; instead of sections there were departments, instead of urban districts there were prefectures. The people of Moscow must have been thinking that since we now had a mayor and prefectures as in Paris, we would soon start living no worse than the Parisians.

Some inhabitants of the city, indeed, did experience a rapid rise in prosperity. Gavriil Popov and Yury Luzhkov, moreover, now not only had power, they also had the pleasant-sounding Western titles of mayor and premier. The new Moscow leaders were the same old bureaucrats and politicians who had headed the city administration before the reform, but it shouldn't be thought that there was no more to the reform than a switch of name. The proclaimed division of power was consistently carried out in practice: the executive branch was fully freed from all control by all responsibility to the representative branch. From now on, the elected organs could criticize the actions of the mayor's office as much as they liked, prove that they were illegal or even criminal, vote to annul decisions taken by the city government—but they were nevertheless powerless. All power was concentrated in the mayor's office, and no one had the right to interfere in its actions.

Even Moscow public prosecutor Gennady Ponomaryov, who protested the mayor's decisions as being in obvious contradiction to the legislation and constitution, was soon to find out what "strong executive power" meant in practice. Illegal decisions were carried out regardless of what was said by representatives of the law of the land or the councils. Protests weren't worth the paper on which they were written; the same went for the laws cited by the discontented. When, at the Moscow government session of July 24, someone referred to laws which were still in force, Luzhkov was genuinely indignant: "What do we have to keep looking at the Constitution for?"

Activists from the democratic movement, who earlier had been Gavriil Popov's faithful and trusty supporters, were shocked by the list of prefects the mayor appointed: Communist functionaries with many-year-long Party service records predominated. He even appointed the former second secretary of the Georgian CPSU Central Committee, Nikolsky, and one of the leaders of the Moscow Communists, Bryachikhin. The liberal press immediately reminded its readers that Nikolsky had been in Tbilisi in April 1989 when soldiers had hacked down unarmed demonstrators with shovels and therefore he could not but be directly implicated in those events. Protests came not only from the ironic and relatively independent *Kommersant*, but even from *Moscow News* which had traditionally supported Popov. They were rather late in the day with their protests, however. For Gavriil Popov had never concealed his sympathy for the old party *apparat* with which he had links going back many years. In addition he had thoroughly assimilated Marx's thought that an idea convinces only when it is based on practical interest.

As an educated man, he knew full well that the replacement of the Communist by the capitalist regime would only benefit those who already possessed both power and connections. He knew that the bureaucracy had long dreamed of converting its illegally seized power into "legal private property," while for the majority of the people such changes would signify at best a partial change of master. Nor had Gavriil Kharitonovich ever concealed his dislike of representative democracy: take, for instance, his article in *The New York Review of Books* on the dangers of democracy. In America this article gave rise to some bewilderment since its author had been represented as a prominent democrat. We, however, had had plenty of opportunity of late to become convinced that our "democratic movement"—or at least its upper reaches—had nothing more in common with the ideas of democracy than the upper echelons of the Communist Party had in common with the ideas of socialism.

But in the final analysis it wasn't the appointment of the old party bureaucrats to the prefectures that did the most harm to the city. Far more frightening was the administrative chaos engendered by the meaningless and irresponsible reforms. Replacing the old district structure with the new municipal regions and prefectures made it impossible to figure out who was responsible for what. Even the agencies of law and order, whose job it was, presumably, to protect the new power from incensed citizens (among others) found themselves paralyzed since they had retained the old district structure which did not tie in with the new administrative divisions.

After geographers, economists, and experts in city management had spent about a year arguing over how best to construct the new enlarged districts, Moscow government officials had simply taken a pencil and traced the new boundaries on the map, guided, they said, by "common sense." Their common sense left much to be desired. As soon as the new boundaries were announced, the city was plunged into chaos. Some regions were missing schools and clinics, others police stations. Some ended up with "surplus" institutions. By the second day of the reform, the boundaries had to be retraced. The prefects had no time to devote to the city's problems—they were too busy arguing over their mutual claims.

Not everyone was discontented. The more administrative chaos existed, however, and the less anyone paid attention to the law, the easier it was to share out the city's real estate. The reform had a positive effect, too, on the rats and cockroaches who, thanks to the new regime, began to wander freely through the streets.

Life got harder, though, for members of the opposition. The mass media which was controlled by the power structure started up a discreditation campaign, attacking Gonchar who, in the space of a few weeks, had gone from being a member of the democratic movement to being painted a CPSU agent. Late one evening, the police arrested Aleksandr Popov on the threshold of his own home. Since he was carrying three boards, he was promptly accused of having stolen them from a building site. They didn't even bother to determine from which site the boards might have been removed. It was immediately established that Popov had gotten the boards from an acquaintance in a neighboring apartment, and that he was being detained illegally, but the very next day reports appeared in the pro-Yeltsin *Rossiyskaya Gazeta* and the Communist *Moskovskaya Pravda* that the socialist deputy had been caught red-handed stealing the boards from a building site. A news item to the same effect was broadcast on TV throughout the country. The discredited deputy took legal counsel, but the investigation took time. All attempts to win an official denial came to nothing since the papers' reports had been based on information from TASS, the official news agency, which could not provide a meaningful explanation as to where the information had come from, since there was no trace of it in the police reports submitted to TASS and the newspapers.

15

YELTSIN and Popov spent some time that spring looking for an excuse for totally doing away with the representative branches of government, but never did come up with anything useful. The Communist Party was decaying slowly, and the process of forgetting it began; the building of the Central Committee of the Communist Party of the USSR in Staraya Square was quiet, cool, and empty as a burial vault. Everyone was fed up with Gorbachev's endless talk of preserving the Union. Members of the Council of People's Deputies protested against the strengthening of the executive branch of government but were powerless to do anything about it.

By July, everyone was out of breath. Politicians of every ilk departed for their vacations. No one could have foreseen how this reprieve would be interrupted.

On the morning of August 19, radio and television programs announced that Gorbachev had suddenly taken ill at his summer house in the Crimea and that the State Committee on the State of Emergency (GKChP) had been formed to take over all the power structures in the Union. Two days later, when the Russian parliament convened, one of the deputies mistakenly referred to it as the "committee on emergencies." This slip expressed the essence of events brilliantly: a state of emergency was never introduced, but there had indeed been an emergency.

It was a strange sort of coup. With the morning announcement that Gorbachev had been relieved of his powers, everyone thought that something major had happened. And while Gorbachev's declared successor, vice president Yanayev, was nothing if not laughable, the "junta" included interior minister Pugo, defense minister Yazov, and KGB head Kryuchkov, all of whom were, without a doubt, to be taken seriously. But their behavior was hard to understand. Communication and transportation services, for some reason, continued to work; soldiers were not armed; Yeltsin was not arrested. The events of August 19 were dubbed a "Communist putsch," but official CPSU structures did not play an active role in them, and the "junta's" pronouncements were ideologically neutral. The putsch plotters had all been among Gorbachev's closest allies— Pavlov, for example, was personally responsible for the economic reforms taking place in the country. Meanwhile, active Stalinist leaders like Nina Andreyeva and Moscow City Council deputy Viktor Anpilov condemned the coup.

Those of us who were outside Moscow when the events occurred and were thus forced to observe the goings-on by following press agency reports were puzzled. So were those who were in Moscow. Activists of the pro-democracy movement, who congregated in response to Yeltsin's appeal to defend the White House, didn't know quite what was happening, either. The coup leaders' military commanders had sent tanks to the White House, albeit without supplies of ammunition. They had not, on the other hand, placed a single armored vehicle by the Moscow City Council building. Portions of the Tamanskaya and Kantemirovskaya divisions were brought in, sans ammunition, with orders to "get to the destination and wait." They would not have been equipped to offer serious resistance if someone had decided to attack them or if there had been mass disturbances.

Armored vehicles were used to block traffic only around the Kremlin, creating a new pedestrian zone, which pro-democracy activists immediately put to use by holding unsanctioned rallies there. There was not a single attempt to force the rallies to disperse. Only Central Television, the Central Telegraph building, and the TASS building were placed under military guard.

Publishing houses and printing plants were not guarded. The rest of the military equipment was idly standing around in the city center. Following Yeltsin's address at nine in the morning and Luzhkov's similar address at noon, the position other Democrats would take was a foregone conclusion: they would not support the state of emergency. Still, the coup leaders did not even attempt to detain key officials with pro-democracy views. Communications services continued to function.

As Kondratov noted caustically, "Instead of seizing power, the putsch plotters were preparing and conducting a press conference."

On the morning of August 19, socialist deputies and the activists working with them gathered at the Mossoviet. A lengthy and fruitless discussion on what was to be done was already in progress. There was no quorum, so it would have been impossible to make any sort of decision anyway. One of the pro-democracy deputies kept screaming something about Yeltsin and a general strike, which no one seemed to be planning to organize. None of the Communists present spoke in support of GKChP, but not everyone was thrilled with the confused and confusing displays of resistance at the White House. Kondratov managed to cool passions somewhat by offering to undertake a legal analysis of the GKChP's pronouncements. From the point of view of jurisprudence, the new regime was illegal and one could with a clear conscience charge the GKChP with rioting.

The quorum that made it possible to make a decision materialized only in the evening in the person of Stankevich, who came, said nothing, and left. But for the purposes of protocol this was sufficient, and a decision was made. A Special Committee of the Moscow City Council was created as a counterforce to the "putsch"; Vladimir Kondratov and Aleksandr Popov were among its members.

Gavriil Popov was out of town on the morning of August 19. He arrived in Moscow quite late. Gonchar was also absent from the capital and knew nothing about the coup. He was vacationing in the Crimea, not far away from Gorbachev's summer house in Foros. Only on August 20, when he returned from a hike in the mountains, did he find out that there was a coup in Moscow. He called the White House. To Gonchar's surprise, he got through right away. Russian secretary of state Gennady Burbulis, who answered the phone, advised the chairman of the Moscow City Council not to rush to get to Moscow but to walk around Gorbachev's summer house and determine what was going on there. Which is what Gonchar did. He determined that what was going on was absolutely nothing: business as usual.

Later Gonchar entertained suspicions that this had been a ploy to keep him from arriving in Moscow in time. Whatever the case may have been, the chairman of the council was absent, as was Popov. Everything fell on Sedykh-Bondarenko, who practically lived at the city council for the next few days; he was assisted by deputy chairman Belov, the Moscow organization's representative in the City Council leadership. It was Belov who signed the Moscow City Council directive for Ekho Moskvy to resume broadcasting when it failed to appear on the air.

The putsch plotters announced that they were shutting down most of the newspapers and reinstituting censorship. Not a single newspaper, however, was closed. All the editorial offices continued to function. They were promised that in the near future all publications would be able to register anew and resume publication. Printing plants were ordered to cease printing most non-Communist and some Communist publications, but no one was really monitoring this.

Ekho Moskvy resumed broadcasting in accordance with the Council directive. "Banned" newspapers encountered no obstacles in continuing to publish, except that they had to reproduce their issues using photocopy and rotaprint machines. The entire leadership of *Moskovsky Komsomolets* sat around the editorial offices in peace, drinking tea, while the job of reporting from the White House square fell to a very young girl for whom it would be good journalistic practice.

Some situations were perfectly ridiculous—as when Pavel Gusev, convinced that *Moskovsky Komsomolets* was not being distributed widely enough, grabbed a huge pile of fresh newspapers and attempted to drag them out of the building and onto the street. He was stopped, not by the putsch plotters, but by his own security guards, who suspected that the editor in chief was trying illegally to remove huge bales of newspaper property.

Despite the evening introduction of curfew, the city saw a citizens' night out. Not only did people walk around as they pleased, but cars drove every which way since the traffic police were nowhere to be found. Although the Kremlin was blocked off, Kondratov and Baranov, in a quest for information for City Council, encountered no obstacle on the way to the residence of the scary "junta." They spent a long time chatting with the officers there.

Gavriil Popov returned to Moscow toward evening. He tried to disarm City Council security and evict the deputies from the building, declaring that in case of attack no one should attempt to resist. When the guards refused to disarm and the deputies refused to leave the building, the mayor left, not to be seen in the Red House again for a long time. Luzhkov, responding to the disturbance, allowed the guards to receive their weapons back—but without the bullets.

In the morning Mossoviet had been surrounded by paratroopers under the command of General Zimin, but by the end of the day they were gone. "The general who was in charge of them had a clear line to Luzhkov," recalls Baranov. "So the paratroopers, working with the police, did not allow anyone except staff members and deputies into the Mossoviet, saying they were acting on the basis of a Luzhkov directive."

Meanwhile, Kondratov and Baranov, having reviewed the Kremlin guard, proceeded to the White House. Here they found almost the entire membership of the Moscow branch of the Socialist Party, the anarchists, and the Greens. After taking a look around, Baranov noted, "We have come here to defend our enemies."

Yeltsin was using the forces he had to defend the gigantic building. In front of the television cameras, standing atop a tank that had arrived to block off access to the White House, facing the barrels of enemy guns, Yeltsin was personally handing out his decrees to the people. Was he that much of an idiot? Or did he need a very large arena in which to demonstrate his personal courage, and was he certain that he would not be either killed or arrested?

Barricades built mostly of metal piping from construction scaffolding and steel armature were going up around the White House. The tanks—without ammunition and with plugged-up barrels—that had crossed over to the side of the Russian government were being placed inside the barricades around the White House. Members of the Russian OMON, armed with submachine guns, were taking places on the first floor. The streets leading up to the White House were blocked with trolleybuses, buses, trucks, and barricades made of park benches, armature, and whatever else was handy. Moscow residents were implored to come to "the defense of the Russian parliament" in the name of Yeltsin. No weapons were handed out—there was nothing to hand out. There was also a catastrophic lack of gas masks and other instruments of civil defense. People who answered the call were assembled in the streets behind the barricades and between the barricades and the White House.

Altogether, according to Kondratov's observations, there were between 15,000 and 60,000 civilians there, depending on the weather and the time of day. Had an attack on the White House been planned, its scenario would have been easy to predict based on past crises in Tbilisi, Baku, and Vilnius: it would have involved the use of tear gas, possibly water cannons, and armored vehicles, which would have squeezed the crowds out. The barriers at the White House would have presented no obstacle for the tanks. Most of these barricades could not have stopped even a light armored vehicle; in Afghanistan these vehicles had overcome more serious obstacles. In the event of such an attack, people who were located between the street barricades and the White House would have had no choice but to climb over the barricades to move closer to the president's residence.

And blood was shed in the early morning hours of August 21, during a confrontation between a relocated military formation and the crowd near the White House. Three people were run over by armored vehicles. At first this incident was declared an attempted attack. A few days later the official propaganda machine was forced to admit that there had been no attack, but now they could talk of a "bloody junta," of "fighting on the barricades in Moscow." Within hours, the defense of the White House grew over with officially recognized legends, much like the Bolsheviks' seizure of the Winter Palace in 1917.

Baranov and Kondratov arrived at the scene of the action a few minutes after the first shots sounded. The armored vehicles under whose tires people had died left the site of the confrontation immediately, but their exit was blocked by the crowd, which surrounded them in the tunnel where they sought refuge. The young soldiers in the military vehicles could not understand what was going on and were scared to death. A while later, the tricolor Russian flag appeared atop the vehicles. Then, to his utter astonishment, Kondratov noticed unarmed people who had made themselves comfortable on the side of the frontmost vehicle. He was even more surprised when he saw who it was. Toward the socialists standing on the barricades, the armored vehicles were bringing Aleksandr Popov, Yury Khramov and the secretary of our faction, Yelena Klimenko.

Here is what had happened. Following the confrontation at the barricades, a group of deputies went down to negotiate with the soldiers and convinced them to surrender. The soldiers and the officers were not exactly understanding what was happening, but they were afraid that they would now be lynched. Basically, the negotiations came down to calming down the nineteen-year-old kids in the armored vehicles, who had lost their heads entirely, and to make it clear to the crowd that the "frightful enemy" against whom they had just been fighting was simply a group of terrified young boys who could elicit only pity.

The shuttle diplomacy ultimately proved successful and everything ended well. There were no casualties aside from the three people run over at the White House. Or, if there were, then they died at other times in other places, and were not reflected in the official statistics. Everyone was especially impressed by Yelena Klimenko, who sat upon the lead car wearing a bulletproof vest and a helmet. A rumor circulating the next day had it that the powers that be were looking for this "legendary heroine" with the goal of giving her a Cross of St. George, a medal of the Tsar's Russia that had now been reinstituted by Yeltsin. It is easy to see that Yelena would not have exhibited particular enthusiasm on the subject of the supposed honor.

There were no other serious incidents during the days of the putsch, unless one counts the occurrence on Lenigradsky Prospect, where three young and very inebriated pacifists attempted to stop an armored vehicle. These bruised heroes of the resistance were delivered to a hospital, where, according to the newspaper *Kommersant*, one of them was found to have a blood-alcohol level of 7.4 percent. Our experts, the newspaper continued, "cannot maintain such a level standing up."

16

THE PUTSCH PLOTTERS fled—but, for some reason, not to Iraq or North Korea but to join Gorbachev in the Crimea, where they were quickly arrested. Yanayev, Pugo, and Kryuchkov's coup had failed. Yeltsin's coup had succeeded. Gorbachev was delivered to Moscow in the capacity of president of a state that no longer existed—in essence, as a hostage of the White House. Communist newspapers were shut down, CPSU buildings were sealed (as were the offices of organizations that had supported the coup, including even the Veterans Union). A few days later Gorbachev ceremoniously declared that he was leaving the CPSU and that its property was to be confiscated and the Central Committee of the party to be dissolved. Russia was starting a new life—a life without Communists, but with Yeltsin and Rutskoy.

The capital's leadership quickly realized that the August events had created great opportunities for it. Representatives of city government were appointed to oversee the press and buildings which had belonged to the Communist Party. The Russian government, meanwhile, was doing the same thing. At the entrance to the Central Committee building in Staraya Square, a group of armed personnel sent by the mayor's office encountered an identical group of people with submachine guns who had been sent by the White House. It came close to a fight. In the end, the representatives of the mayor's office chose to retreat.

The mayor's office made some other mistakes as well. In the August rush, Aleksandr Popov was appointed to represent city government to *Moskovskaya Pravda*, the old publishing house of the capital's Communists. Instead of attempting to bring the publishing house and the newspaper of the same name under the control of the mayor's office, he started defending the editors' interests. Yury Khramov was given the task of commanding the Moscow OMON forces sent to guard the publishing house. Once the crisis was over, though, the government stopped making such mistakes.

Once the "victory of democracy" had been officially announced, mobs of overjoyed fans of the Russian government got to work taking down monuments and attempting to demolish party offices. The latter was intercepted decisively, since the victors themselves needed the offices. So the defenseless monuments, which no one had any intention of guarding, took the brunt of the people's righteous anger. They were not so easy to pull down, however. While the crowd easily succeeded in pushing over the statue of Sverdlov that had been placed in the former Teatralnaya Square during Brezhnev's period of stagnation, Marx, who had been built in the same square in the first few years after the revolution, managed to stand his ground. The crowd worked long and unsuccessfully to push over the monument to Feliks Dzerzhinsky, the founder of the Bolsheviks' secret service, in Lubyanka Square. Had the mob succeeded in toppling him on their first try, the many tons of Iron Feliks would doubtless have broken through the ground and paralyzed the metro station located underneath. Fortunately, this did not happen. Luzhkov sent construction equipment over, and the lengthy and expensive liquidation of the monument began.

Another part of the crowd set off to throw Lenin's mummy out of the mausoleum but, fortunately, got distracted by something along the way. The sociologist Mark Shmit, the founder of the country's first anticommunist party—the Democratic Union— sent out a call for defenders of the late leader, and volunteers quickly began to gather around the mausoleum.

Soon after the events between August 19 and 21, Moscow was

hit by an epidemic of peculiar suicides. The first to leave this life was General Pugo. By some strange coincidence, when Russian KGB workers went to arrest Pugo, they took along the economist Grigory Yavlinsky, who proceeded to describe what happened in an article in *Moskovsky Komsomolets*. General Ivanenko, who headed the arresting team, easily reached Pugo by phone and asked him to wait at home. Pugo's building was surrounded by Russian KGB workers anyway. But when the group arrived at its destination, it was Pugo's father-in-law who opened the door, whereupon Ivanenko for some reason asked him, "Has there been an accident?" The old man answered in the affirmative, and the group ceremoniously proceeded into the room where Pugo and his wife lay in puddles of blood.

The wife was still alive, but it was clear that she was severely wounded. Without undertaking an investigation, KGB workers immediately declared the incident a suicide. Everything would have been fine had it not been for the handgun, which, for some reason, was sitting on a night stand at the other end of the room—which Yavlinsky let slip. Not only that, but he let it slip not orally but in print, on the pages of a newspaper with a readership in the millions. A new version was immediately announced: Pugo had been shot by his wife, who then committed suicide. If Yavlinsky's account is to be believed, however, first she somehow managed to hit herself in the face a few times. But that's details. As soon as the new version was announced, Pugo's wife passed away in the Kremlin hospital. On this occasion, Aleksandr Shubin, the leader of the greens, could not help but making a mean joke: "They may not shoot very well sometimes, but they sure give good medical care."

September saw the appearance of a new official version—this one, apparently, final. Lisov, prosecutor general of Russia, told the press literally the following: "Pugo shot himself in the stomach. His wife went up to him, took the handgun, and shot herself. But then she was able to put the handgun on the night stand, go over to her bed and lie down next to her husband." What an incredible zeal for order in a dying person! But Pugo, apparently, was not so worried about how he was going to appear to Yavlinsky. For some reason, the general "shot himself" not in uniform but in sweat pants.

Gorbachev's adviser Marshal Akhromeyev hung himself right in the Kremlin. Shortly after the burial, a group of especially active Democrats opened his grave and extracted his uniform.

At the very height of these events, I bumped into Vasily Shakhnovsky, the administrative director of the mayor's office, as he was coming out of Gonchar's office. This man, usually very happy and cheerful, was pale as a sheet.

"What's with him?" I asked when Shakhnovsky had left.

"Today they announced that Kruchina committed suicide," Gonchar answered.

Kruchina had been administrative director of the Central Committee of the CPSU. It was announced that he had jumped out a window. For some reason, he picked not the highest balcony but the fifth floor. And he had an odd way of falling, too: instead of landing right beneath his own window, he fell some distance away, as though he had taken a running start before leaping. And no two people "killed themselves" the same way. One shot himself, another hanged himself, still another jumped.

The theory that Kruchina might have been murdered immediately popped up in the media, along with the idea that Kruchina must have been eliminated by "his people" because he could have known about secret CPSU money. In reality, such things rarely went through the hands of the official administrative director. But he was privy to an entirely different kind of information. Political contacts that do not leave traces in the administrative system do not exist. Somebody needs to be issued a pass, someone else has to formalize a business trip, order a car, accept a package and so forth. Even if the administrative director does not know anything, he can guess.

It is not surprising that Kruchina's fate worried Shakhnovsky. He was not the only person who had reason to worry about his health. Kryuchkov, a professional, had taken preemptive measures immediately. Following his arrest, he somehow managed to give a television interview in which he communicated, first of all, that his health was perfectly fine and his mood was wonderful. So there appeared to be no reason for him to die of a heart attack or hang himself in jail.

17

AUGUST 1991 served to lift all limits on the behavior of the ruling circles. The ceremoniously announced triumph of democracy over the "bloody junta" was accompanied not only by the liquidation of Communist newspapers, a wave of denouncements, and an attack on the still-functioning agencies of representative government, but also a true bacchanalia of redistribution, which began when the winners started divvying up the take. The Communist Party apparat had long since hidden away most of its money in commercial banks and had been quietly privatizing by investing in private companies. It would have been meaningless to speak of hidden party money, since money was moved into secret accounts not in order to continue the fight underground but to finance private entrepreneurial activity. There was no "hidden" money: there was stolen money. Still, the liquidation of the CPSU yielded quite a take for the winners in the form of real estate worth many millions of dollars.

The takeovers of buildings were not limited to party property. There were urgent searches for putsch "collaborators" who might have something to be taken, too. They started in on the leadership of the Writers Union, dominated by "enemies of democracy": there were some tasty pieces of real estate to be had here. But since "patriotic writers" refused to vacate their property just because they had not condemned the GKChP's actions in time, Prefect Muzikantsky organized a siege of their building. They even closed the Veterans' Unions, where there was almost nothing to take. Along the way, they took buildings that had no connection at all to agencies of the old regime. For example, the publishing house Russky Yazyk [Russian Language] had a building that someone in the city leadership must have had his eye on because it was taken away. This publishing house puts out foreign-language dictionaries, which are perhaps superfluous in a society where people can no longer even communicate reasonably in their native language.

The redistribution was accompanied by obscene squabbles between the governments of Russia and Moscow, not to mention the fact that the distribution of such a rich inheritance among new owners could not help but create fertile ground for corruption. We'd never had a problem with corruption—in the sense of any serious obstacle to bribery and embezzlement. For several years already, the relevant divisions in the internal affairs system had been paralyzed and laws had not been applied. But now quantity was transformed into quality. It was called "privatization." Gavriil Kharitonovich repeatedly—and truthfully, after a fashion—underscored that this was its democratic variety: theft was an option not only for the few with access, as under the old regime, but for anyone who could hustle.

It seemed like Moscow and Russian authorities had decided to prove Prudhon's famous thesis that "property is theft." One would be hard put to find a Moscow structure whose privatization was not accompanied by all sorts of suspicious machinations.

The process of privatizing residential properties was a grand example of the city authorities' democratic principles. The issue was discussed countless times in the mayor's office and the City Council, with new solutions being proposed every time. The dead end was evident. The administration's and the Council's inability to find a version of the plan that was at all palatable was not caused by squabbles within the administration or by political intrigue. It was simply that a large portion of the city's residential resources was not ready to be privatized. There was simply no way to split up huge apartment buildings into hundreds of little real estate holdings without injuring the residents themselves. They would then be left alone to face the monopolies of utility services, federal taxes that would rob them, and the city authorities' unwillingness to do anything at all to rejuvenate the capital's residential resources. How to privatize—free of charge or for pay, and if for pay, then how to evaluate the worth of the apartments—all this remained a mystery. Meanwhile, the privatization of apartments continued in full swing even in the absence of final decisions. And this was when the miracles began.

Having announced in the fall of 1991 that there would be paid privatization of apartments, the mayor's office sent a letter to the finance ministry requesting permission for citizens to use money from frozen compensation accounts for this purpose. These accounts belonged to people who kept money in the state savings bank almost a year before Gorbachev and his new prime minister, Pavlov, started to amuse themselves by forcing all their subjects to exchange all their old hundred-ruble and fifty-ruble notes for new ones in the space of two days. Having promised the people that prices would rise and there would be inflation, Gorbachev had made a generous gesture by ordering to have the Savings Bank open special accounts equal to 40 percent of the citizens' savings. These special accounts, however, were frozen until 1995.

Like most of the account holders, Gorbachev and Pavlov knew perfectly well that by that time the coveted 40 percent would equal nothing. The money had to be put in circulation in some way before hyperinflation truly began to spiral. After the Democrats' victory in August, that would not be too long in coming.

Thus Gavriil Popov and his administration found a way to save the money in the special accounts. By directive of the finance minister, the special accounts were unfrozen for those who were privatizing their apartments. But this remarkable fact was never publicly announced—probably in the interests of preventing a mob scene. The information was disseminated to those "in the know." And now dozens of high- and medium-level Moscow bureaucrats went and privatized their apartments, having withdrawn their coveted 40 percent. Now came the most responsible part of the procedure: as soon as the core mass of the city functionaries completed privatization, the mayor's office reviewed its own decision and announced that apartments would be handed over to citizens free of charge. After this, the lucky ones who had paid for privatization with money from the special accounts arrived at the mayor's office en masse, and their money was given back to them in cash. All this happened in October; on January 2, the Russian government announced the liberation of prices, and within a few weeks all our savings had vanished like smoke.

The privatization affair and the divvying up of party property were not the only profit-making opportunities. The "humanitarian aid," massive amounts of which began coming into the country after August, was no less valuable in this respect. All the newspapers, regardless of political orientation, cursed the thieves of humanitarian deliveries, but the journalists were tactfully quiet about the fact that there was no way Russian and Moscow authorities were unaware of the large-scale theft of aid even while they were begging the West for it. No one even tried to establish control over the ways in which aid was used.

It had been agreed that a significant portion of the humanitarian aid would be sold by private entrepreneurs at commercial prices. This was supposed to stimulate the formation of capitalism. For their part, the authorities made sure that almost nothing made its way into the state retail system. Moscow administration minister Karnaukhov personally told European Community representatives that meat must be delivered uncut, with bones; this gave the butchers yet another opportunity to show their famous skill at using the scales to cheat customers, while store directors got a chance to show how they sell the good cuts through the back door, and thieves were given the opportunity to pass the meat off at the market as the "production of independent farmers." The point was not just that the ways of cutting meat are different in Russia than in Western Europe; the point was also that, in accordance with the standards set by the Moscow Medical Epidemiological Station, meat that arrived already cut was not allowed to be sold at markets.

City authorities had plenty to do. It was thanks to their efforts that city streets saw the appearance of healthful young men who looked like karate fighters or the British Queen's Grenadiers who sold Dutch hot dogs, Italian spaghetti, and Swiss chocolate at a price that exceeded the average consumer's resources by a factor of merely five or ten. As for non-average consumers, they had finally been given the opportunity to see the market's invisible hand in the flesh—and they were quite pleased with its appearance.

There were missteps, of course. The most unpleasant one happened in the winter, when the capital authorities accidentally sent a plane full of British beef, intended for Moscow, to Murmansk. The beef was cut according to the mysterious Western European customs and was clearly no longer suitable for sale in the marketplace. In addition, the price of meat in Murmansk continued to exceed that in Moscow by about 40 percent—despite the rising prices in the capital. The authorities declared the meat rotten and rerouted the plane north, where this same meat was deemed quite suitable for consumption. At this time, several doctors from the Moscow Medical Epidemiological Station tried to protest, saying that they'd also found the goods to be of fine quality and had unsuccessfully tried to impress this upon the leadership, which, as we say, knows better.

When this story made its way to the television screen and the printed press, it aroused much public interest, but as always, efforts to hush it worked. But Karnaukhov clearly had to pay for the British beef with his portfolio: when the capital cabinet was reorganized, Karnaukhov's name had disappeared from the list of ministers.

18

AN ATMOSPHERE of fear and uncertainty settled over the country. A witch-hunt began, ostensibly because it was necessary to eliminate the Communist threat. Committees on unconstitutional activity were formed; even their members referred to them as "committees on denouncements." Anatoly Baranov called them the Senator McCarthy Memorial Committees. When calls for reports on unconstitutional activity on the part of officials were broadcast on radio and television, a wave of signals rolled into all sorts of agencies. The Moscow City Council's commission received from 300 to 400 reports a day. Yury Khramov publicly, on the pages of *Moskovskaya Pravda* ("The Moscow Truth"), called for the commission's archives to be destroyed. "Not even historians will have any use for it," Yury kept saying. "Unless somebody decides to write a history of Russian denouncements."

Some liberal newspapers published calls for a stop to the attacks on civil liberties. *Literaturnaya Gazeta* published reports on a concentration camp for the putsch plotters that was allegedly going up near Tver, and on prohibitions and persecutions that would certainly not benefit a democracy. Even the editor in chief of *Nezavisimaya Gazeta*, Vitaly Tretyakov, wrote that "a paradoxical situation is taking shape: the independent press may die as a result of... the victory over the putsch plotters and the liquidation of the CPSU."

The liberal politicians also felt discomfited, but unlike the journalists, they looked for protection by declaring their devotion to the leader. Gavriil Popov was nervous. He had been late for the coup; when he had arrived, he had not been able to comprehend the situation right away and had ordered the OMON squad guarding the Mossoviet disarmed.

Despite Popov's outstanding achievements in the area of privatization and administrative reform, the mayor of Moscow turned out to be an ideal candidate for the role of scapegoat. In an effort to demonstrate his patriotism, Gavriil Kharitonovich could find nothing better to do than to suggest that Yeltsin be awarded the honor of a Hero of the Soviet Union. The television cameras immediately broadcast Yeltsin's crooked smile for the entire country to see.

Now Popov might be made to pay for his old anti-Yeltsin article in *Moscow News* and his attempts to manipulate the "great leader" in his own interests. But even that was not Gavriil Kharitonovich's biggest problem. All his actions to the contrary notwithstanding, he was simply too much of an intellectual for Yeltsin's circle. Whatever else one could say about him, he'd actually read some books and knew a few things about political economics. This fact alone was enough to make him a black sheep among the new political leaders. A different kind of people were coming forward. Yeltsin proteges who had begun their careers in the party apparat in the provinces were quickly pushing intellectuals out of the way. Russian state secretary Gennady Burbulis and his cohorts were fast getting accustomed to the halls of power. These people had not read any books, but they acted decisively, without regard for laws and the Constitution.

The strategy of the mayor's office in this situation was the only correct one: it was necessary to place faithful people in key places in the agencies of repression as soon as possible, before an out-and-out conflict with the higher authorities developed. Constant confrontations over the divvying up of property contributed to building tensions and were likely to lead to very serious conflicts. Speaking crudely, what was liable to happen shortly was expressed in Lenin's famous question: "Who'll take whom?" That is, who'll take whom and put them all in prison first?

Popov attempted to get on solid ground with the Russian president while at the same time continuing his struggle against the Russian cabinet of ministers. This strategy quickly proved fruitful. On August 28, 1991, Yeltsin signed his Decree Number 96, which rescinded the powers of the Moscow City Council which had been guaranteed by the Russian law on local self-governance. It took away the Council's control over city property and limited our input into budgetary questions. It handed control over the city's personnel policies to the mayor's office as well as control of the law-enforcement agencies. In essence, what was left to the deputies was the right to free use of public transportation and the right to gather regularly for fruitless discussions of decisions of the mayor's office that we had no way of influencing.

On the morning of August 30, when the contents of the decree were made public, Aleksandr Popov approached me in the deputies' cafe.

"We have talked with Gonchar. We decided that if the decree is not validated because it is unconstitutional, the entire Council has to resign collectively."

"Sure," I responded, as though what we were talking about was familiar and routine business. The Council's imminent demise no longer evoked any emotions in me.

The next day was the Day of the City. Around noon, Gonchar barged into his own office beside himself with rage: in addressing city authorities, His Holiness the Patriarch of All Russia first mentioned the deputy mayor, then the mayor, forgetting about the Council and its chairman altogether. Apparently, this fairly ridiculous incident was, for Gonchar, the straw that broke the camel's back. He spoke angrily and harshly.

"We must make a statement now. If we do not resign, they will remove us anyway. But at this point we can take the initiative and retain our sense of dignity."

After thinking a minute, Sedykh-Bondarenko agreed.

Gonchar was nearly screaming. "We have no other choice!"

There was no debate. Gonchar's assistant Mikhail Trushin and I went into the next room and drafted the Council's resignation letter. This took no more than twenty minutes.

The letter said that in light of the fact that the country was seeing a restoration of administrative-authoritarian power in a new guise, an elimination of representative government, and disregard for the law, we could no longer carry out our constitutional duties and were collectively resigning. At the same time we were demanding that the laws of the Russian republic be observed and new elections scheduled.

Now we had to convince the deputies. Those who had chosen to make the Council their place of work now had salaries of 700 rubles a month (seven times the average wage); no one wanted to sacrifice his status.

The extraordinary session in September decided against taking such a radical step. Instead, the Moscow City Council turned to its usual protest strategy and adopted its own resolution on the distribution of power in the city. It limited the mayor's authority and rejected Decree Number 96 as being illegal.

Whether it was legal or not, it was being observed. And we had no authority. The case of General Komissarov once again became a symbol of the stand-off between representative government and the new regime. Appointed back in November 1990 by the Moscow City Council, this out-of-favor general was still not allowed to take his job as the head of Moscow police.

At first the mayor's office tried to keep this position in the hands of General Myrikov, who had replaced Bogdanov not long before the August events. During the putsch the general had screwed up when, in an August 20 communication, he had directed all district police stations to follow GKChP directives to the letter. Nonetheless, the mayor's office continued to defend the general confidently—at least, until the administration had found a suitable replacement for him among their people. Contact with GKChP, which had cost many people their careers, did not create any difficulties for Myrikov. Bureaucrats from the mayor's office insisted that in carrying out the putsch plotters' orders, the general had not committed any serious crimes and had kept the mayor's office constantly apprised of his actions.

The general did not, in fact, end up doing anything illegal. The only surprising thing was the strange selectivity that allowed strict measures to be taken in some cases—as with the officials of the Writers Union, who could at most be considered "accessories in spirit" for publicly recognizing the GKChP—whereas in this case a person who gave orders, whether or not they were fulfilled, could be absolved of guilt.

Since explanations from the mayor's office did not satisfy the deputies and it was impossible to accomplish anything through normal parliamentary means, members of the Committee on Legality employed a tried and true tool and started their second hunger strike. This time they occupied the Council's Red Hall. The hunger strike was well-organized and had the support of a majority of deputies.

Poor Myrikov enjoyed the protection of the mayor's office only as long as it took to find a replacement. The shuffling began, however, not with the police, but with the leadership of the Moscow KGB directorate, where counter-intelligence professionals were replaced with the mayor's allies. Popov's assistant Yevgeny Sevastyanov became the new head of the KGB, and Moscow City Council deputy Aleksandr Sokolov became his deputy (we immediately took away his council membership). Thus, at the helm of the Moscow KGB we now had professionals who knew the political situation well, knew who could be a threat to the new authorities, and were very well informed on the activities of opposition groups.

Only then did Popov turn to the police. Appointing Komissarov was not even an option—his arrival on the job could lead to investigations into corruption and big problems for the Moscow government. The first person advanced for the position of head of the GUVD was the economist Krasavchenko, and for the position of his deputy, Vladimir Bokser, who headed the National Guard of Moscow, an ad hoc militia formed by the mayor's office after the August events. Strictly speaking, the National

Guard fit the definition of an "illegal armed group," and was financed through unidentified means to boot. By appointing Bokser deputy director of the GUVD, the mayor's office would have killed two birds with one stone: placing its people in the GUVD and making its illegal formations a part of the official law enforcement system. But this did not go over. After evaluating the situation, Krasavchenko declined the appointment, thus also canceling the appointment of his deputy.

Advanced in Krasavchenko's place was Arkady Murashov, an expert in high-temperature physics. He was also a people's deputy of the USSR, and since the Union and its parliament were living out their last days, it was necessary to find jobs for activists from the pro-democracy bloc who were losing their status as parliament members.

Witty *Kommersant* journalists wasted no time asking if, in light of Murashov's profession, it would not have been better to appoint him the city's fire chief. If Popov felt such a great need to make the city police chief a significant political figure, then he could have done the same for the fire chief.

Events were taking a serious turn. Contrary to the Russian administration's expectations, Russian Supreme Soviet deputies decided that they did not want to betray their colleagues from the Moscow City Council. It was too obvious that by supporting the new authorities in their drive to undermine the position of the capital's council, the Russian parliament would have paved the way for its own dissolution. In September Ruslan Khasbulatov, chairman of the Russian parliament, threatened the deputies by saying that if they demonstrated a "lack of tact" in relationship to Yeltsin, then "the president can address the people through television, and then the defenders of the White House will simply throw us out of here."

The Moscow deputies' second hunger strike could have had a tragic ending. Sedykh-Bondarenko developed a bleeding ulcer and was taken to a hospital, where he was immediately operated on. New deputies kept joining the hunger strike. Even those of us who did not support using a hunger strike as a weapon declared that we were ready to join the hunger strike. Huge letters spelling out "Hunger Strike" were painted on the Mossoviet windows; fliers hung on the walls kept us informed about what was going on. Rallies were held regularly and kept getting bigger, attracting 5,000 to 6,000 people.

On September 19, the Russian Supreme Soviet declared that the Murashov appointment had been illegal and demanded that Komissarov be allowed to start his job. For the Russian deputies, Moscow had become a front line of defense. The longer the Moscow City Council was able to hold on, the more time the Russian parliament would have on its hands—although it was not entirely clear what that time would be used for.

The hunger strike was stopped, but it was too early to celebrate. Just a few days later, the authorities launched a counter-attack. On Wednesday, September 25, a rally organized by Gavriil Popov and his allies was held in Sovietskaya Square in front of the Mossoviet. The Council held a long discussion on whether to allow Popov to speak from our balcony (one mayor had already used this very balcony for calling for the dissolution of the City Council). The majority voted to allow him to speak. No other decisions were made or measures taken.

All the leaders of the "pro-democracy" community attended the rally, including such idols of the liberal intelligentsia as Aleksandr Yakovlev and Eduard Shevardnadze. Speeches singing the praises of the Moscow and Russian administrations alternated with calls for the dissolution of the Council. "Hang the hunger strikers!" declared a banner raised proudly above the crowd. "Hang them! Hang them!" chanted the defenders of democracy. The leaders of the new Russia stood proudly on the stage, listening to tributes to themselves and threats to their enemies.

Activists who had been assisting the hunger strikers thought about creating a large and beautifully executed pirate flag as a joke. After surveying the mob, though, they decided not to push it: it would have been too dangerous.

It was a bit frightening to stand in this crowd. Nonetheless, the deputies pinned on their deputies' buttons and descended into the square to stand there. People insulted them and threatened them, but the buttons had a magic effect. People were afraid to come too close to them.

"I am feeling for the first time that wearing this button is a real honor," noted Aleksandr Popov. Looking at the banner calling for violent punishment for the hunger strikers, he added, "If they touch Babushkin, I don't know what I'll do with them. That would mean war."

That same day, Komissarov was removed from his position by Dunayev, the Russian minister of internal affairs. Murashov, the new commander of the Moscow police, ceremoniously set off for Komissarov's office. He was accompanied by the minister himself, the new head of the KGB, Sevastyanov, Gavriil Popov, Yury Luzhkov, and bodyguards. But he was not able to occupy the cabinet. He was met at the door by deputies of the Moscow City Council.

"You don't have the right to enter," deputy Tsopov declared. "Your actions are illegal."

"What you are doing is illegal and unreasonable!" Luzhkov screamed in response.

"It may be unreasonable, but it's legal," said Tsopov. "If you attempt to enter, I will use my military-issue weapon. As an officer, I have the right to do that," Tsopov reached into his jacket pocket and produced a document guaranteeing his right to carry and use weapons; with his other hand, he reached into the back pocket of his pants. This proved sufficient. The entire procession, bodyguards included, turned around and ran for its life. The mayor of the city along at the front, mumbling curses; the internal affairs minister of Russia followed. There was no gun in Tsopov's back pocket.

When Gonchar found out what happened, he grew very concerned. The leader of the Council sensed that things had gone too far, and he didn't want to take further risks. But by now we could not and would not retreat.

A gap between the Council chairman and the more radical faction among the deputies appeared during these days and grew wider. The weakness of the Council, which was unable even to submit its resignation, had convinced Gonchar that the

Council would have to make concessions. The socialists, like many independent deputies, drew the opposite conclusion: that it was necessary to assume more extreme positions if we were going to accomplish anything at all. This division dealt a final blow to the Moscow City Council's ability to act as a serious opposition force. Following the confrontation on Petrovka [street, where police headquarters are located], we expected trouble. Naturally, we didn't have to wait long. The blow was returned the next day. Speaking before DemRossiya members, Mironov, whom Popov was planning to appoint deputy director of the Moscow police, named the two most "harmful" hunger strikers: Khvatikov and Babushkin. That very evening, three unidentified persons attacked Andrey Babushkin in his own apartment.

The doorbell rang. The front-door intercom was broken and the light in the stairway turned off.

When Babushkin opened the door, he saw an athletic-looking young man.

"Is this Apartment 74? Your window is broken." Babushkin was about to object that his window was not broken at all but did not have time to say anything. The stranger grabbed him by the hand and the head and dragged him out into the stairwell. Two more men appeared and started beating Andrey on the head with a water pipe. Andrey started screaming.

Fortunately for him, two of his assistants were in the apartment and came out into the stairwell. The attackers fled. Babushkin was taken to a hospital.

19

WHEN MUSCOVITES went to the polls in March 1990, they believed in the vision of a rejuvenated city, in honest officials, and in freedom. Over the course of the following year and a half, the capital turned into a city of broken roads and bitter residents, a city where everything functioned less and less well daily but cost more and more.

There was an odor of easy money about the capital. There was also an odor of blood. Calls for creating a law-based society were replaced with the slogans of "strong authority."

There was no one to blame because everything that was happening in the city—the violence and corruption that ruled it—were, at least formally, the result of the residents' own free choice. And if we had been able to retain this freedom, we would have been able to create a different, more honest kind of rule for ourselves. The only problem was that the people sitting at the top at that point, the ones enjoying the fruits of the great victory, knew this too.

Stopping in the hallway at the Mossoviet, Yury Khramov shook his head: "This all resembles October just too much." What happened on August 19 had little in common with the democratic revolution of February 1917—it was more like the October Revolution backwards.

The mayor's office was systematically taking over city buildings, now evicting not only the old party organizations but also organizations formed between 1990 and 1991. The Moscow Property Foundation, formed by the Moscow City Council to attempt to monitor privatization, was placed under siege. Electricity was turned off, and the OMON blockaded the building at Kropotkinskaya 17. The mayor's office wanted to use it to house its own foundation for the support of small business. On October 16, the police of the Southwestern Administrative Region, clad in helmets and bulletproof vests and carrying nightsticks and weapons, stormed the building of the disobedient Cheremushki District Council. Deputies were dragged out of their offices and had their arms broken. Formally, these actions were based on orders to take over the space of the old district committee of the CPSU in this building, which had long since been taken over by the Council.

The Mossoviet itself was facing the threat of a takeover by the mayor's office. Repeated attempts to evict the Moscow City Council and place it in what used to be the V. I. Lenin Museum, which had once belonged to the City Council, were unsuccessful. The deputies had no intention of leaving the Mossoviet, especially since the Historical Museum was also trying to lay claim to the Lenin Museum building.

In the end, it was the mayor's office that left the Mossoviet. The move was accompanied by a scandal. The Moscow City Council's technical personnel complained that in leaving the building, the mayor's staff took the furniture, the chandeliers, and even went as far as unscrewing the light bulbs and tearing switches out of walls.

Every day in October brought new reports of building seizures, evictions of lawful occupants, and fights. But the agencies of repression were just stretching before taking serious action.

Mobs of enthralled supporters of the new regime were carrying pictures of the leader around the city, toppling monuments, and demanding cruel punishment for the "enemies." Yevgeny Yevtushenko, who became famous for his poems about Lenin, was now writing about the new leaders, singing praises of the defense of the White House:

The tanks' conscience is awakened.
Yeltsin climbs atop a tank.

His poetry about Lenin was better.

After August DemRossiya faced a crisis of its own. No longer needed as an anticommunist movement to consolidate power, it was gradually being supplanted by the Movement for Democratic Reform (DDR) founded by Gavriil Popov together with former nomenklatura workers, and the nationalist People's Party of Free Russia, headed by Rutskoy. The two organizations were competing for the spot of official state party, vacated as a result of the CPSU's demise.

The lack of unity among the winners—Burbulis and Shakhray were at war with Khasbulatov, Luzhkov, and Silaev—gave the dissidents a chance. Sensing danger, left-wing groups started working on forming a united organization. Socialists, anarcho-syndicalists, trade union activists, and the left-wing opposition from the ranks of the old Communist Party began working together to create the Party of Labor. For his part, speaking at the DDR's Political Council, Gavriil Popov warned that left-wing radicals would soon take to the streets with the people in order to counteract reforms, and that this was something Murashov and Sevastyanov would have to work on. The KGB and the police now had a new job: fighting left-wing radicals, a good many of whom had immunity as council deputies.

Soon thousands of people did take to the streets. On October 23 the Moscow Federation of Trade Unions called the working people to a rally to protest the social and economic policies of the new Moscow and Russian authorities. The organizing committee of the Party of Labor also supported the rally. The mayor's office tried to ban the rally, using the same arguments that Moscow City Council Secretary Vinogradov once relied upon in his attempts to ban or reschedule rallies held by the non-Communist opposition.

Despite the attempts to ban it, the rally did take place. The authorities had given in at the last minute. About 50,000 people gathered in Manezh Square, and people stood on the sidewalks of neighboring streets listening to the speakers. There was wet snow and a piercing wind. Sensing that the participants would not last long, Moscow Federation of Trade Unions leader Mikhail Shmakov tried to wrap up after an hour. But the crowd did not want to disperse.

When City Council deputy Ilya Zaslavsky, speaking on Central Television on behalf of DemRossiya, said that the defenders of the White House had fought for Yeltsin and Russia, he mentioned "democracy" only in third place. Indeed, no one was giving democracy the decisive spot, and no one had any plans to do so. The defenders of the White House were no doubt sincere people, decent people inspired by great ideas. But the same could be said about those who seized the Winter Palace in 1917. Both groups of people were young. Neither had any idea what their actions would lead to.

Very soon many of the people who had responded to Yeltsin's call to come to the White House had to ask themselves, "Was this why we went to the barricades—so that bureaucrats could combine politics with business while Yeltsin's circle divides the property of the CPSU?"

Millions of people in Russia had fought for democracy. What we got was Yeltsin.

The new leader's triumph would not have been complete without removing from the stage his old mentor and competitor Mikhail Gorbachev. As long as the Soviet Union was preserved, Gorbachev also continued to exist politically—and this was not something the country's other leaders could live with. The issue was solved simply and quickly. Meeting with the Russian and Belorussian authorities in Belovezhskaya Pusha, Yeltsin took only a few hours to reach a deal that dissolved the Soviet Union and offered the added bonus of shipping Gorbachev off into political nonexistence. Having evaluated the situation and realized the futility of resistance, the president of the Union State preferred to concentrate on his personal problems. After taking a stroll through the Moscow stores and depositing over a thousand rubles there in the space of a few hours, the former ruler of the great empire declared, "That's it! Time to make dollars. And use them for myself."

The Yeltsin regime was actively involved in creating its own mythology; it planted its new symbols everywhere. People dressed up as the Tsar's Cossacks started showing up in the Moscow City Council buildings; to our surprise, we even recognized a Moscow deputy—he had joined the Moscow Cossacks. What the Moscow Cossacks are, remains to be discovered, since history tells us of the Don, Kuban, Yaitsk, and other Cossacks but is stubbornly silent on the subject of the Moscow Cossacks.

The Tsar's double-headed eagle was also returned to its place. Since—for now—we had a republic, the eagle was often depicted without its crown. The resulting look was rather ragged around the edges, which gave the *Kommersant* humor writers the idea of joking about the "Chernobyl broiler" anointed as the symbol of the new Russia. In March 1992 the Russian Supreme Soviet deputies spent an entire day trying to choose an appropriate bird for the state seal. Three versions were presented to them for consideration, but they rejected them all, calling the eagles "salmonella-like."

These democratic activists were especially outraged by the absence of the crown, the orb, and the scepter from all three designs. Oleg Rumyantsev, a socialist democrat, even declared, "This is not a seal: this is a disgrace to the Russian Federation and a sign of disrespect for historical traditions." He demanded that all three large imperial crowns be returned and the wings lifted. Someone suggested that Rumyantsev advance his own design, but he kept complaining: "The Parliament is going to edit the eagle in such a way that all that will be left of this roast chicken will be the legs and something unpalatable."

Some of the Democrats complained that the legislative agencies were still in the hands of Communists, who would certainly vote against the crown. Others noted that the eagle had come out somehow underfed and plucked—to which the specialists in heraldry objected that the state seal should, after all, correspond to reality.

"In general," noted the head specialist in heraldry, Georgy Vilinakhov, "we are seeing a violation of the logical sequence. Russia is still a republic. First it has to be transformed into an empire, and then we can decorate the eagle with imperial crowns. Otherwise it would look pretentious."

To my mind, this schizophrenic double-headed bird was actually a very suitable symbol for the new state. The ruling bureaucracy was trying as hard as it could to become a real, legitimate bourgeoisie, but it did not for a minute stop being, in essence, a corrupt bureaucratic mafia. It dreamt of putting its new privileges firmly in place and legalizing them, restoring what it could of the old regime's structures—not the pre-October, pre-Bolshevik regime, but the pre-February imperial monarchy.

All great revolutions have gone too far in forging ahead, making it inevitable that the revolutionary regime would die, a new oligarchy resembling the old would appear, and in the end there would be a restoration. That is what happened in England in the seventeenth century; that is what happened in France. In this sense, Russia was no exception. The only trouble was that too much time had passed between the revolution and the restoration. Too little was left of the old regime, so our bureaucracy was restoring not the old regime but rather its own idiotic concept of it.

History was repeating itself as a farce, like it is supposed to. But history does not stop at restorations. If we recall the past again and look at what happened in England and France, just as the revolutions were followed by restorations, the restorations, as a rule, were followed by "nice revolutions," by the Restoration of the Revolution.

A utopian vision of general happiness and a joyful future cannot inspire a nice revolution, which has much more limited but more easily accomplished goals—to restore the most valuable revolutionary achievements and values undermined by the restoration. For us, this means not only social guarantees for the population and returning to the people the property created by the people's labor and stolen by the bureaucrats, but also guaranteeing basic democratic freedoms. This is the historical challenge of the left wing in Russia today.

The first experiment in democracy in seventy years was not

particularly successful. But it was not wasted. The hopes of the people who gave their voices to DemRossiya in the spring of 1990 were betrayed, but still, no one can stop our struggle—our struggle for a rejuvenated city and a liberated country that belongs not to bureaucrats and the moneybags but to us at last.

20

THE CAPITAL awaited the first post-Communist winter with trepidation. The Russian government promised to mark the year 1992 by liberating prices; the Moscow authorities promised that there would be enough coal to last almost the entire winter. Judging from experience, the city dwellers understood that "almost" meant there would not be enough and that "liberating the prices" meant everything would get more expensive.

On November 24, the city cafeterias received shipments of meat that had been purchased at "negotiated prices." As a result, the price of a worker's lunch tripled in one day. There was outrage at the factories. Low-level trade union functionaries were making phones at local agencies and at the Moscow Federation of Trade Unions ring off the hook with pleas to "do anything at all, or else there will be a riot." The meat was replaced with vegetables in short order, placing the workers on a vegetarian diet in an attempt to disguise the price hike. By the evening of November 25, trading at "negotiated prices" was stalled, but it was already too late. The trade unions demanded that the government enact a number of social security measures that had been promised but not enacted (not that anyone had really planned to enact them). Picket lines formed around the mayor's office and the White House; transportation workers were threatening to strike; and a Moscow-wide state of strike readiness was planned for December 25. City authorities ordered the pickets to disperse; organizers, who included Moscow City Council deputies from the Labor faction, were arrested. Nothing happened: the capital's police refused to carry out the orders and General Postoyuk, responsible for maintaining order around the Red House, announced to the crowd of protesters that no one would be detained. "I've been pushing for a salary raise for a long time too," the general added.

On Saturday, December 14, news that Gavriil Popov was leaving the job of mayor spread for the first time. Earlier, while answering questions about the future of the capital's administration, Yeltsin had noted that Gavriil Popov was "physically tired." Anyone familiar with the ways of the bureaucracy knew this meant it was not the mayor's health that was shaky, but his position in Russia's ruling circles. Finally, Gavriil Kharitonovich himself announced his resignation at an official press conference. As was his custom, he wasted no time in blaming all of the city's misfortunes, including his own imminent resignation, on the Council deputies who would not let the administration do its job. Popov's many attempts to abolish or dissolve representative government in the capital had failed. The councils—weak, deprived of real power, helpless in the face of the arbitrary actions of the administration—had still managed to outlast the mayor.

During the fall months, the capital, like the rest of the country, had been consumed by an orgy of absurdity. Representatives of the new regime had promised us that, having done away with communism, they would "bring us out from beyond the looking glass," but we continued to wander among warped mirrors. The triumph of the winners took on insane but fairly traditional form: anything that could be was repealed, renamed and reorganized. They began with the time. Having repealed the time-by-decree that had been instituted in the country by the Communists [what amounted to permanent daylight savings time], they managed to move the clock's hands in the wrong direction. As a result, it started getting dark at three in the afternoon, and night and day became confused.

Names of streets and Metro stations continued to play hide-and-seek. The first wave of name changes was followed by a second. Some stations were renamed twice in a row: Kirovskaya [named for Sergei Kirov, a revolutionary] turned first into Miasnitskaya [named for a nearby street] and then into Chistiye Prudy [for a nearby pond]. Sherbakovskaya [named for Aleksandr Sherbakov, a prominent 1930s Communist] first became Novo-Alekseyevskaya [New Alekseyevskaya, referring to the location] and then, for some reason, simply Alekseyevskaya. A third wave of name changes was being readied, which would affect the vast majority of perfectly ideologically neutral names. The list of new names published in *Kuranty* shocked even the intellectuals who were normally devoted to the authorities. The final straw was the decision to move the Kaluzhskaya metro station by canceling this name in one place and awarding it to another. Imagining the suffering of future passengers trying to find out where exactly it was they were going, even *Izvestia* commentator Otto Latsis called this decision sadistic.

The senseless name changes were supplemented by insane appointments. When pro-Yeltsin activist Lev Shimaev, who had once served time in prison for murder and then became a decent rally organizer, suddenly appeared as the director of an arts center to be created on the site of the famous Sandunovskiye Baths, even the Moscow bureaucrats who had seen it all sensed that something was going awry. Shimaev's appointment was opposed by bathhouse devotees, who organized a protest movement. Thanks to Anatoly Baranov, they immediately became known as the "Sandunista Front."

Any historian who uses the mayor's office archives to study our era will surely get the idea that the mayoral authorities experienced something of a mental disturbance as a result of all the events. How could a person who does not suffer from a split-personality disorder start corresponding with himself? That is exactly what happened when Gavriil Popov the editor in chief of the journal *Voprosy Ekonomiki* ("Issues in Economics") addressed a request to Mayor Popov, who fulfilled it himself, while vice mayor Yury Luzhkov corresponded with the entrepreneur Yury Luzhkov, the head of joint-stock company Orgkomitet, and in the end always reached agreement with him.

Vice President Aleksandr Rutskoy was granted the rank of general following the August events. During his tour of Siberia he called vice premier Yegor Gaidar and his colleagues "boys in pink pants." The moniker immediately stuck. The newspapers repeated Rutskoy's words in unison—while, of course, distancing themselves from the general and even making lots of complimentary comments in Gaidar's direction—but unable to resist the temptation to dwell on the color of his pants. Without even knowing it, the general doomed Gaidar's reforms to ultimate failure with this one phrase. The ministers to whom the label had stuck were no longer able to accomplish anything because it was difficult to take them seriously.

In this situation, the public did not even show much trust in Popov's imminent resignation. Rightly so. Immediately following Popov's announcement of his resignation, a delegation of highly placed city civil servants met with Yeltsin and got everything they wanted. Popov rescinded his resignation announcement, while Yeltsin stopped referring to the mayor's poor health or his being "tired."

In place of the mayor's resignation, a rearrangement of the Moscow administration was staged. Luzhkov announced that he was leaving the position of prime minister and was immediately given a new appointment. He was made the prime minister of the new Moscow government.

The main casualty of the reorganization, as it turned out, was Karnaukhov, a veteran of Moscow retailing. He had survived a lot during his time in the leadership—not only dozens of scandals and newspaper exposes but also inexpensive meat, cheese, and milk. The goods, it seemed, came and went through the back door, but Karnaukhov stayed. But Karnaukhov proved unable to survive humanitarian aid. The scandal with British beef apparently exceeded what the capital's current leadership would allow. Karnaukhov's well-known carelessness in such matters also played a role. At one point there had been trouble with sugar that appeared at warehouses out of nowhere and disappeared from there into nowhere. The persistent Anatoly Baranov had appeared nearby out of nowhere and described it all in *Moskovsky Komsomolets*. Now, after the beef had been declared unfit for human consumption, it turned out that Moscow hygiene experts were definitively insisting that it was fit for consumption; meanwhile Ken Livingstone, the former mayor of London, in Moscow by invitation of the Party of Labor, was threatening to launch a Parliamentary investigation into the matter in England.

Karnaukhov may have been lost, but something was found. *Moskovsky Komsomolets* editor in chief Pavel Gusev was appointed minister of propaganda in the Moscow government. The obscene-sounding title was proper reward for a person who had spent an entire year conscientiously trying to prove to the city that everything good that happened in the capital happened thanks to the administration while all the trouble could be blamed on Moscow City Council deputies, Communists and left-wing radicals.

At the same time as Gusev's appointment, compensation was handed out to other journalists from all sorts of publications who had written articles praising the mayor of Moscow and his administration. Since there weren't enough jobs for everybody, some just got money. This caused something of a scandal among colleagues who had not been similarly remunerated—and some of the deputies indignantly waved payment receipts in the air, attempting to protest the direct attempts to "buy the press"— but what difference could that make? Gusev wasted no time in his new job.

Gusev had never been a professional journalist. The first time I met him was when, in his capacity as secretary of the Krasnopresnensky regional Komsomol [Union of Communist Youth of the USSR] committee, he was inducting me into that glorious organization. It was still under his leadership that I was later purged from the organization for "antisocial activity"—distribution of the samizdat journal *Levy Povorot* ("Left Turn").

Thus the government was reorganized, propaganda problems successfully resolved, and all we had left to do was await new victorious communiques informing us of the blossoming of the city, the eradication of the communist, socialist, and Moscow City Council foes and the final liberation of the market from all sorts of control (as well as goods and, most likely, customers).

The worse things got in the city, the more frequently receptions and banquets were organized by the authorities. Champagne kept pouring. According to the newspapers, the reception held on the occasion of the close of the winter Olympic Games in Albertville outdid all others. The Moscow City Council's White Hall shone with charming women's smiles. Presenting gifts to sports heroes, the Moscow mayor said with feeling, "Anything can happen in life. If you ever need anything, don't be shy—come to us, and we'll help you." As he uttered those words, the newspapers reported, Gavriil Kharitonovich for some reason had his gaze fixed on the figure skater Marina Klimova.

21

INASMUCH AS the activities of the city elders were not limited to the capital but were developing on a Russian and even a world scale, the corruption that ruled the Moscow mayor's office was becoming known around the world. The words "mayor's office" began to go hand in hand with the word "mafia." Nosy Western journalists who kept running into the mayor of Moscow in such places as Rome and Paris could not resist the temptation to dig for details.

Gavriil Kharitonovich was not the least bit embarrassed by their questions. "The mafia problem," he declared on French radio, "is being artificially inflated by the opponents of reform, and lately it has become totally obnoxious, if I may say so. Anyone who fights against the market and the transition to capitalism is depicted as a fighter against the mafia. In our country, where there are ten different bans that apply to any normal economic activity, what is called the mafia is mostly normal activity."

In the hopes of embarrassing the mayor in the eyes of the Muscovites, the communist newspaper *Glasnost* reprinted this interview. But Popov was not in the slightest embarrassed by his words. Furthermore, a few weeks later, he developed his ideas in the utmost detail on the pages of *Argumenty i Fakty*.

Reading the interview, one found out that the mayor was categorically opposed to "extortion" but had nothing against a reward given by mutual agreement. This can, of course, be called a "bribe," he conceded, but it would be more accurate to refer to it as "commission." He had always been embarrassed when he did not know how much he was supposed to give in order to thank a person. In America, the mayor of the Russian capital had learned that it is customary to give 15 percent of the amount of the deal, although he thought that Moscow conditions warranted no more than 10 percent.

From now on, the issue of "reward" was clear. Anyone who wanted to "reward" the mayor or another civil servant from the Moscow government now knew exactly how much he was supposed to give. Especially since, as Popov insisted, in America it costs more. I suspect that U.S. prosecutors would be interested in learning which of Gavriil Kharitonovich's colleagues in that country shared such valuable information with him. Anyone who is more or less well acquainted with Russian literature could easily see that, having assumed the position of city ruler, Gavriil Kharitonovich—himself a great fan of Gogol—was starting to reason just like the town governor in "The Inspector General," who, as we know, also didn't accept bribes, preferring "gifts."

Foreigners, less attuned to the subtleties of the situation, could not understand the difference. During his visit to Moscow, Ken Livingstone, noted that by English law Gavriil Kharitonovich should have been imprisoned long ago and that his public statements could be considered confessions. Gavriil Kharitonovich took offense and wanted to file suit against *Nezavisimaya Gazeta*, which printed the Livingstone comment. Later, he thought better of it and withdrew the claim. As long as Yeltsin and similar Democrats were in power, no one was going to touch the Moscow city ruler.

The only thing Gavriil Kharitonovich, who preferred to deal with foreign companies, did not take into consideration was the limited means of the domestic business community. Konstantin Borovoy, who headed the Russian Goods and Raw Materials Exchange (RTSB), had declared publicly on several occasions already that the mayor's office wanted too much and that

Russian entrepreneurs were unable to pay such large bribes (commission, that is). At first Borovoy and his cohorts threatened to declare Moscow an unfavorable zone for entrepreneurs. After a few months, seeing no change for the better, he held a press conference in which he accused the Moscow government of out-of-control corruption of the sort possible "only in a feudal state." According to Borovoy, apparently, under capitalism the government should charge less. Unlike Popov, however, Borovoy did not specify how much.

Frightening headlines appeared in Moscow newspapers in the middle of April: "Businessman Accuses Moscow Government," "Entrepreneurs Demand Resignation of Moscow Government," and so on. It looked like Borovoy had declared war on Popov. The papers quoted Borovoy's accusations: "The city's executive government is gradually becoming intertwined with criminal structures, creating a unique mafiosi network that controls the city's life." "The best buildings and historical landmarks have been sold off and rented for nothing for lengthy periods to foreign firms." Popov, of course, was not the only one accused. Experts representing the Moscow Entrepreneurs Convention criticized contracts into which Zaslavsky's team had entered in the Oktyabrsky region. On April 9, Borovoy's group even appealed to the Muscovites to demand the resignation of the government by boycotting the city authorities and their representatives.

Borovoy had weighty reasons to hold grudges against Popov and Luzhkov. At one point Luzhkov, according to Borovoy himself, had given a gift to RTSB by placing the Moscow social security fund in the RTSB Bank instead of a state or municipal bank. The deposit amounted to over 100 million rubles that had been raised through the commercial sales of cigarettes following the tobacco crisis. This was big money in those times, especially since RTSB was just beginning to do business. Where the interest on that money went, we can only wonder. One way or the other, all the parties in this deal should have been satisfied.

But then something did not go as planned. The money was taken out of the RTSB Bank and moved to the Moscow People's

Bank. What is worse, the Moscow Goods Exchange (MTB), RTSB's main competitor, started to gain speed under Popov's patronage.

In response to the criticism from Borovoy and his cohorts, Popov gathered together his entrepreneurs, who declared in unison that everything was in order with Moscow's mayor's office and the administration. Here the key figures were MTB president Vasilyev and Zagulin, a young businessman. In his time Vasilyev had worked under Zaslavsky in the Oktyabrsky region, where he had headed the Directorate of Communal Property (UKOSO), made famous by its shady machinations. Zagulin had carved out a place for himself in the history of the Moscow university as the Komsomol functionary who headed the surveillance service; it was probably then that he became close to Popov, who headed the ideologically significant economics department.

The mayor's allies were not acting all that militant. They called the mayor's attention to the "necessity of examining Mr. Borovoy's commercial projects." Being practical people, they knew full well that it was not a good idea to fight and that if Borovoy was this insistent, then they could just share a part of the take. Their signal was interpreted correctly, and the Borovoy protests ceased.

The mayor's troubles did not end there. If the Moscow prosecutor's office could be controlled (just in case, the Moscow prosecutor was dispatched on a business trip to Paris), then foreigners were a source of endless trouble. The French law enforcement authorities launched a criminal investigation into the leadership of the joint-stock company SARI, Gavriil Kharitonovich's main partner in the deal in Gagarin Square.

But this could not stop the Moscow government. The triumphant ceremony of laying the first stone in the building of the complex in Gagarin Square was scheduled. Honored guests were invited—including President Yeltsin, who demurred. Alas, this too resulted in a blunder: a crowd of indignant local residents crashed the ceremony. Two women, one of whom turned out to be a deputy of the regional council, simply lay down in the pit intended for the first stone. The police refused to remove them: deputies' immunity still meant something to them.

After arguing with the crowd, the organizers of the ceremony decided to retreat. The empty pit was left gaping in the middle of the square. The first stone had not been laid, but neither had the pit been filled.

22

AFTER THE New Year, the Russian and Moscow authorities started enacting economic reforms in earnest. Prices were finally entirely let go and rose to heights out of customers' reach. Taxes rose even higher than prices. State enterprises started to suffocate under the new taxes, which, by the ruling circles' own admission, were directed specifically against the state sector. The private sector also encountered some difficulties—but only the entrepreneurs who tried to produce something had problems. Those who were living off speculation, thievery, and corruption were doing just fine.

Even the Westernized part of the Moscow intelligentsia that had been loudest in saluting the triumph of the new regime was having second thoughts. "Today the person who does not have dollars has realized that he does not belong in Moscow. The mayor's office, meanwhile, has confirmed that the center of town is a place for the rich," the remarkable writer Grigory Gorin wrote in *Nezavisimaya Gazeta*. "Pieces of a living city cannot be auctioned off without taking into consideration that there are indigenous traditions, even if they seem odd to foreigners.... But these are our traditions and our city. For a long time we lived under the dictatorship of the Communists, but now we have found out that life under the dictatorship of business people is no better. They couldn't care less about what country they are in."

To the majority of regular "Soviet citizens" who were not overly concerned with philosophical problems and were not members of the CPSU, the People's Front, or the Writers Union, the lessons of the new regime were even more apparent. Nostalgia for the Communist past was growing in the capital. At least under Brezhnev there had been affordably priced goods, one could go out into the street without fear, and even if bribery was no less widespread, at least the amounts were smaller.

The devotees of the Communist idea, having recovered from the August shock and having gotten rid of the hated Gorbachev leadership, were once again coming out into the streets. The Russian Communist Workers Party (RKRP) was the vanguard of this movement, and its leader in the capital was Deputy Viktor Anpilov.

Anpilov did not hold much sway on the Council, even among members of the Moscow bloc; his speeches, full of revolutionary appeals and threats in the direction of the Democrats, could hardly have elicited the support of listeners. But this speaking style proved quite effective at the pro-Communist rallies of the winter and spring of 1992. The mob, bitter and confused, at least half made up of the old participants in pro-democracy rallies, was consumed with hunger for vengeance. No slogan elicited more enthusiasm the calls for punishing the people guilty of bringing the country to catastrophe, of lying to the people and dooming them to poverty and extinction. It was impossible to explain to the mob that in order to punish the guilty it was necessary at least to have a strategy for coming to power. Anpilov and other activists of his ilk devoted little energy to thoughts of this sort, instead repeating, like a spell, magical phrases like "The people's anger will do away with the anti-people government."

Every two or three weeks Anpilov called the people to yet another rally. The same old speakers, speaking one after another in the order to which they had grown accustomed, proclaimed the same old slogans. The rallies drew up to 100,000 people—and sometimes more—but these too were the same old people. For most of the city's residents, these appearances, like the less and less attended counter-rallies held by DemRossiya, had become a fairly boring routine. Despite the discipline that had become customary over the years in the Communist movement, a certain level of exhaustion and apathy could be felt among the rally participants as well.

Gavriil Popov came out with bloodthirsty speeches in which he argued for severe measures against the "red threat." Just as in the spring of 1990 and 1991, this upped the ante and provided a fresh stimulus for antigovernment activity. The democratic press, for its part, was united in demanding that the authorities put an end to any and all opposition activity. "If the Anpilovs and the Kagarlitskys say anything that is antigovernment or anti-constitution, then use the apparatus of repression that any state has at its disposal. If pensioners and students come out into the streets and start storming the White House—which, of course, is really impossible—then the police and the OMON are equipped to prevent that," *Kuranty* wrote on February 6, 1992.

March 17 was to be the climax of the stand-off. The supporters of a restored union scheduled a congress of the People's Deputies of the USSR for this day—the anniversary of Gorbachev's meaningless referendum on the fate of the Union. If the congress had a quorum, it would be able to accept Gorbachev's resignation and proceed to elect a new president of the USSR, who would also be the commander in chief of the armed forces and could demand that everyone follow the orders of the restored lawful authority. Naturally, no one would follow the new president's orders, but at least they could count on a minor civil war or on the introduction of a state of emergency.

On Red Army Day, the Moscow government's forces not only brutally broke up yet another Communist demonstration but prevented even war veterans from placing flowers on the grave of the unknown soldier. The young officers of the law beat up confused old men, and ripped up and stomped on the red flags under which their fathers and grandfathers had won the most horrible war in the history of Russia.

From all appearances, Gavriil Popov was satisfied with the actions of the police for the first time in many years. Prior to this, he had publicly reproached Murashov for his indecisiveness several times, threatening layoffs and expressing indignance that demonstrators encountered no obstacles in violating the numerous bans invented by the mayor's office. All these reprimands, threats, and warnings finally had an effect; on February 23, the police had finally shown what they were capable of.

If the same thing had happened on March 17, it would have been fair to expect heavier consequences. Popov, however, insisted on severe measures but did not want to take responsibility. In a position paper published in *Kuranty*, the ruler of the capital declared that since the Communists' efforts to resurrect the Soviet Union were unconstitutional, the rally should be dispersed and its organizers arrested. But, he continued; this decision had to be made by the Supreme Soviet of Russia. And if the Supreme Soviet did not make the decision, then Popov was going to allow this illegal rally to take place.

After reading the mayor's statement, members of the Moscow committee of the Party of Labor decided to apply for a permit to hold our own rally. In our application, we said that since the capital government had promised to brutally break up the Communist demonstration in advance, we were similarly taking advance action by applying for a permit to hold a rally of protest against the brutality. Since the law demands that applications be made ten days ahead of time, the Party of Labor was making its request exactly ten days in advance of the predicted event.

The Supreme Soviet was not stupid enough to follow Popov's advice, and did not ban the rally. The Moscow City Council refused to take up the question of the rally altogether. The mayor's office was satisfied with banning the Party of Labor rally on the basis that there was not and would not be any attempt to break up the Communist demonstration.

Everything went ahead in a peaceful and boring manner. The congress of the People's Deputies of the USSR did not manage to gather even a semblance of a quorum, and turned into a regular forum for infighting among the supporters of a resurrected Union. The rally was also quite ordinary, even though the organizers had dubbed it a national vigil. A tiny "vigil bell" was raised onto the stage, where it produced a funny little ring from time to time. The chairman of the Liberal Democratic Party Vladimir Zhirinovsky circled the square in a truck, yelling something into a microphone. What he was yelling could not be heard because the organizers' sound system was far stronger than his and drowned him out entirely. But he kept going around and around as passersby stopped to rubberneck and laugh.

After this, they stopped breaking up rallies. Not only did the authorities realize that regular Communist rallies were no threat to them (most likely, they already knew that), but figured out that it was becoming more and more difficult to scare people effectively with the "Communist threat." Having failed to frighten Muscovites with the ghost of Anpilov, the new authorities got us with boredom and squashed us under the burden of daily worries. The "liberated" prices continued their fast ascent as the standard of living fell. We kept kicking and paddling in an attempt to stay afloat. People stopped having the time for rallies and politics. The new regime could celebrate victory once again. But for how long?

Gavriil Popov, endowed as he was with a keen political sense, probably knew that he should not stay in the position of mayor much longer. In June, just a few months after he was granted yet another round of extraordinary powers, he resigned once again, this time offering virtually no explanation for his action. This time his resignation was accepted. By Yeltsin's decision, Luzhkov was immediately appointed to replace Popov.

Thus Moscow was left without Popov. As the sole proprietor of the capital, Luzhkov started out by threatening to confiscate all unpainted and unrenovated buildings. This had an immediate effect: streets in the center of the city were transformed. As for the social sector, here Luzhkov took only one initiative: he personally supervised the construction of a little bridge connecting the old and new zoos. Luzhkov made a personal appearance at the opening of this structure and posed for photographs, showing how concerned he was about the development of the Moscow infrastructure.

23

NOT ONE of the organs of authority established in Russia during the perestroika years survived, intact, to the end of its appointed term. The representative bodies in their turn were finished off with Yeltsin's televised address of September 21, 1993. Rarely in history has there been a coup prepared so ineptly and so openly. Yeltsin violated the constitution so flagrantly that there could be no talk of his having "made a mistake" or "exceeding his powers." The Congress of People's Deputies and the Supreme Soviet were dissolved. Laws were replaced by decrees.

A fable about "free elections," to be held in December for a new parliament, was hastily prepared for public opinion in the West. Half of the deputies in the upper house were to be appointed by Yeltsin himself, and the obligatory turnout of 50 percent of voters was lowered to 25 percent. The parliamentary mass media were swiftly shut down, and decrees were prepared outlawing trade unions and strikes. Elections for local administrative heads were banned. Western politicians cheerfully supported the overthrow of the Russian constitution, seeing in this a real triumph for freedom.

The opposition was not able to raise objections. Control over television was tightened still further. "The Parliamentary Hour," the only uncensored program in Moscow, was taken off the air. The parliament's press organs, the newspaper *Rossiys-*

kaya Gazeta, and the journal *Narodniy Deputat* were shut down. The nationalist newspaper *Den* was also banned, but quickly re-registered itself and again began appearing. The only remaining uncensored mass media were the newspapers *Pravda* and *Nezavisimaya Gazeta* and the St. Petersburg television program "600 Seconds." No one had any doubts that if Yeltsin's coup succeeded, they would share the fate of "The Parliamentary Hour."

The presidium of the Moscow City Council met only a few hours after Yeltsin delivered his television speech. Members of the anti-crisis team established after August 1991, members of the commission on legality, and representatives of the factions crowded into Gonchar's office together with members of the presidium.

Everyone was waiting for Gonchar's reaction. For several months he had been making regular concessions, trying to defend at least the remnants of City Council's influence. But Gonchar was now unwilling and unable to retreat further.

"There are things to which I cannot reconcile myself under any circumstances," he explained. On the morning of September 22, the Moscow City Council voted overwhelmingly for a resolution condemning Yeltsin's coup d'etat. As in August 1991, the anti-crisis team set to work.

The same day, thousands of people gathered in the White House. Most of them had also been there in August, but this time Communists joined them. Encountering familiar faces in the corridors of the parliament, people embraced, rejoiced at meeting old friends, and joked. Someone suggested creating the title "Twice Defender of the White House." Others suggested that from now on the defense of the parliament would become a traditional popular festival, observed every two years. No one yet realized that what was to happen this time would be different from what had happened in August 1991. Then, everyone had been waiting for tragedy, and what had happened had been merely farce. Now they were waiting for another farce, but what was beginning was a tragedy.

Supporters of the parliament lit campfires beneath the walls of the White House, while the government waited for the Supreme Soviet to capitulate. The authorities cut off the telephones; then began intercepting cars belonging to the parliament on the streets; then ringed the building with militia and interior ministry troops; and then turned off the electricity, the emergency systems, the fire sprinklers, and the heating.

Outside the building, political meetings were continually going on. All parties and all tendencies were here. Some speakers shouted obscenities, some quoted Montesquieu. Communist and Christian Democratic groups stood side by side with centrists, socialists, and anarchists. There were even thirty or forty fascists, who were naturally shown every day on the official television.

Most of the people taking part in the meetings were not members of any party. The newspapers spoke of pensioners, but the people by the walls of the parliament were mainly young. During these days I spent a lot of time wandering around the city. There was one kind of crowd around the commercial kiosks—carefree, noisy, garishly dressed. A crowd of another kind—intense, serious, dressed in worn clothing—was by the walls of the White House. Here was working Moscow. People came after work, simply to hear the latest news. They were not interested in the impassioned speeches of the orators, but simply mistrusted the television reports, and wanted to find out what was really happening. Around the parliament, campfires were burning and political arguments were taking place, boiling over at times into fistfights.

The blockade around the parliament was drawn tighter. Vehicle access was blocked, and supplies of fuel and food could no longer be brought in. The building was ringed with troops from the Dzerzhinskiy Division, but every day people succeeded in getting through. Sometimes they managed to bring fuel and food with them. Although food was needed in the White House, people also fed the soldiers in the cordon.

On the night of September 27, the blockade was finally made impenetrable. Not even medical personnel were allowed into the White House. Around the building rows of street-cleaning vehicles and water cannon were backed up by fully armed special forces troops. The area was ringed with razor wire like a concentration camp. Even mounted police appeared on the scene. Every few minutes, appeals from Yeltsin to the defenders of the parliament were broadcast over loudspeakers. Anyone who surrendered was promised security and a high-paying job in the presidential apparat. Gennadiy Sklyar answered over a megaphone on behalf of the White House staff: "You're judging us according to your own standards. But we're principled people, and we'll fulfil our duty to the end."

Several thousand people remained in front of the cordon, hoping that so long as they were on the scene there would not be an attempt to storm the building. They even managed to seize one of the street-cleaning machines and to stop two trolleybuses. Since they were going to have to stay there a long time, people collected money and bought provisions. All the foodstuffs were placed in one of the trolleybuses. Seeing this, the OMON attacked the crowd and recaptured the trolleybus. They chased the people back a few dozen meters, and ate the food.

When the cordon around the parliament building was tightened, a total of 119 deputies were unable to enter. They established a coordinating committee which met in the building of the Krasnopresnenskiy Regional Soviet, declaring that they would continue to work there until they were reunited with their colleagues in the White House. Television promptly reported that they had gone over to Yeltsin.

The Moscow city government stationed a squad of armed OMON members on the lower floors of the regional soviet building. They entered the vestibule wearing plush leather jackets over their bulletproof vests, armed with automatic rifles and carbines—just like the characters in American movies. You could have killed an elephant with the carbines. They were met by unarmed deputies, young activists from left-wing organizations, and a few journalists. Young women asked to be allowed to hold the carbines, or to try on the bulletproof vests. The invaders were clearly nonplussed.

"So who are you?" people asked them.

"We're the Moscow OMON."

"Well, go upstairs, the Riga OMON is waiting for you."

Several dozen members of the Riga OMON were in fact among the defenders of the White House. This thought did nothing to raise the spirits of our guests. Nevertheless, the new arrivals received good-natured treatment. Not knowing what to do, they killed time reading opposition leaflets and explaining to those around them that "everyone" needed the OMON. "When you come to power, you'll need us too," they said. This squad soon had to be replaced.

I spent almost all that day going around the lines of the cordon, and then working with the coordinating committee. When I went out onto Krasnopresnenskaya Street late in the evening, several thousand people were marching along it in the pouring rain, chanting, "All power to the soviets!" There were no streetcars in sight. Colonel Viktor Alksnis marched in front of the column, giving an interview to an Argentine journalist with a bandaged head.

From the left, interior ministry forces appeared with shields and clubs. They tried to cut the demonstrators off from the regional soviet building. "Colonel, give your order!" shouted the demonstrators, appealing to Alksnis. A former military engineer, Colonel Alksnis hesitated a little, and I thought, he seemed confused. But then he gave his order. The civilian crowd executed a flanking maneuver and surged around the troops from the right, preventing them from massing themselves between the regional soviet building and Krasnopresnenskaya Street.

"This is how a civil war begins," I thought.

However, for a civil war to begin, there must at least be civilians in the country. The September coup showed the weakness of a state that was incapable of crushing the resistance of the regions and even of dealing with a few hundred deputies and a few thousand opposition activists. But it did not show the wretched weakness of civil society.

Few people actively supported the coup, but the bulk of the population remained totally indifferent to what was happening.

Moscow during these days presented a strange spectacle. In

one area of the city, barricades were being built, special forces detachments were beating demonstrators with rubber clubs, and the White House was ringed with armored personnel carriers, razor wire, and thousands of armed people. Meanwhile, only a few dozen meters away, a lively street trade was going on. Cafes and restaurants were operating, and people were hurrying about their business, looking on indifferently as young men in bulletproof vests made short work of defenders of the constitution.

For all that, the resistance kept growing. Every day, several thousand people tried to break through to the White House, which they spontaneously renamed the "House of Soviets." They were beaten and repulsed, but others came in their place. On Tuesday evening the first barricades appeared at Krasnaya Presnya, and on Wednesday there were more of them. Activists from opposition organizations stopped trolleybuses and placed them across streets. This occurred mainly on the Garden Ring Road. On the third day of these events Muscovites were already joking that the trolleybuses no longer went along the Garden Ring Road, but across it.

The Garden Ring Road was the most popular place for building barricades, but not the only one. On Wednesday evening, a barricade was built next to the Belorusskiy train station. A detachment of the OMON, hurriedly dispatched from the Garden Ring Road, got stuck in a traffic jam on Tversky Street. The OMON troops were forced to get out of their vehicles and to run along the street. To do this in bulletproof vests, with weapons and full equipment, was no mean feat. When they finally reached the barricade, no one started fighting them; people simply laughed.

During the first week of the blockade, laughter was our strongest weapon. Everything was done with a good deal of merriment, and despite the dramatic character of the events, people were surprisingly good-natured. At one point Boris Kravchenko, a correspondent for the labor information center KAS-KOR, approached a group of young people who were building a barricade. He was astonished to find that the crowd was carrying the car of German labor attache Frank Hoffer. "Don't touch this car!" Kravchenko shouted. After a short discussion, the barricade builders put the car back where it had been.

The demonstrators went up to the cordon and talked to the OMON and the militia. As the rain poured down, the people in the cordon were soaked to the skin, their faces mournful and helpless-looking. At the head of a crowd of about a thousand people, deputies of the Moscow City Council of the regional councils tried to go through to the White House. The interior ministry troops were ordered to beat the demonstrators. The deputy to the Russian parliament Oleg Smolin, who was blind, was unable to dodge the clubs and received two blows—first on the back, then on the head. Then, standing in front of the cordon, he spoke to the people who had just beaten him. The soldiers listened in confused silence. Many of them took leaflets from the demonstrators.

Andrey Babushkin was arrested by the militia—illegally, since the Moscow City Council had not been dissolved, and he retained his immunity. But when Babushkin's colleagues from the Council, standing on the opposite side of the militia lines, heard of what had happened, many of them could not suppress a smile. Between 1988 and 1989, Babushkin had been arrested several times. The militia knew him well from demonstrations on Pushkin Square; they had evidently seized him out of habit. In any case, he was well known to the militia for another reason as well; as a deputy, he had been concerned with problems of the organs of law enforcement, seeking to set aside apartments for militia officers and helping them resolve a wide range of social problems.

"Let Babushkin go!" shouted the crowd.

"We know who he is," people answered from the cordon.

A few minutes later Babushkin appeared. Someone gave him a megaphone, and he delivered a fiery speech to the militia. Babushkin is not a bad orator, and they listened to him. When it was explained that militia's Lieutenant-Colonel Kopeykin had seized Babushkin's deputy's card and was refusing to return it, laughter broke out on both sides.

"Kopeykin, give Babushkin back his deputy's card!" shouted the demonstrators.

"What do you want a deputy's card for, Colonel?" The colonel emerged from the ranks and began trying to justify himself. The militia members hid their faces behind their shields to conceal their smiles.

Over the megaphone, I said, "Of course, you're not going to lay down your clubs now, you're not going to let us through to the White House, and you're not going to come over to our side. At any rate, not now, because the revolution hasn't started yet." Here people in the cordon again began to laugh. "But as long as we're standing here facing one another, and they haven't given you the order to beat us up again yet, let's talk for a while and try to understand why this has happened. You're defending Yeltsin's reforms. Some people are doing well under these reforms. According to police figures, there were six Rolls Royces in Vienna in 1991. After a year of our reforms, the number of Rolls Royces has doubled, and all of these new cars belong to Russians. Maybe you get to ride in these cars? Anyone who has a Rolls Royce, raise your club."

Then the crowd and the cordon agreed to step back a pace and form a free corridor. When both lines had retreated, someone from the crowd shouted: "There, you see how easy it is to take a step closer to one another!"

The troops were replaced. By the end of the second day of the blockade, the authorities had been forced to bring reserves to Moscow from other regions; the troops were demoralized and unreliable. The commanders were above all anxious not to allow contacts between their people and the demonstrators—they had to keep an eye not only on the demonstrators, but also on their own forces. The tactics changed; people were simply not allowed to gather and to enter into dialogue with the troops. At Barrikadnaya metro station, any gathering of more than five people was dispersed. Even lines at kiosks were dispersed. Everyone was driven into the metro, even non-demonstrators who lingered at the entrance. Then some people came out again, and everything was repeated. The OMON began to go down into the metro and to beat people right on the platform. Bewildered passengers scattered in all directions, trying to avoid the blows. It is amazing that no one was pushed onto the tracks. The injured by this time numbered in the dozens. Colonel Alksnis was taken to the hospital with a fractured collarbone and concussion. One militia officer was crushed by a colleague in a fatal accident while dismantling a barricade.

Throughout two weeks of confrontation, despite the violence of the authorities, the demonstrators did not display aggressiveness. "We don't have anything but umbrellas, so why are you so scared of us?" people asked from the crowd. Not a single kiosk was overturned, and not a single store window was broken. A few cars were overturned, but not one was set on fire. The only business to suffer any particular damage was a very expensive French boutique situated between the barricades of the White House defenders and the militia cordon; the shop was left without customers, closed down "for inventory." It appears also that neither the militia nor the defenders of the parliament had the money to buy the latest Paris fashions.

On Saturday, the situation changed. Stones were thrown at the OMON. Prior to this, the demonstrations had been remarkably peaceful. But a week of frequent confrontations with the "forces of order," of beatings and tension, had done their work. On Smolenskaya Square the demonstrators drove off the OMON, but thanks to Gonchar's intervention, passions were quelled.

On Sunday a new demonstration took place. After assembling on Oktyabrskaya Square, several thousand people made their way over the Krymskiy Bridge to the House of Soviets. This time, the covering forces of the militia were unexpectedly weak—only three lines in all. The streets were not blocked by trucks, and there were neither mounted militia, nor water cannon, nor metal barriers. Many participants in the demonstration began to feel that something was wrong. The militia were behaving abnormally—they were standing idle. The situation was all the more bizarre since the militia during the previous few days had not shown the slightest restraint.

However, few of the people who had gathered were able to analyze the situation. Seeing the weakness of the cordon, the crowd rushed toward the White House and broke through with unexpected ease. Firing broke out from the mayor's office. Even Radio Liberty, which can hardly be suspected of pro-communist sympathies, reported that the Yeltsin forces were the first to open fire. After the first people had been killed and wounded, the scene on the square in front of the mayor's office became one of total chaos. A section of the militia and OMON opened fire on their own forces, and crossed over to the side of the demonstrators. The mayor's building was seized. Some of the people who had been guarding the building were driven onto the upper floors, but they were not molested further, merely remaining trapped at the top of the skyscraper. The obstructions around the White House were removed, and the triumphant crowd filled the whole space around the parliament building.

At 3:40 p.m., Rutskoy addressed the demonstrators thronging around the White House, calling on them to occupy the television center at Ostankino. Several thousand people, of whom only a few dozen were armed, promptly set off in this direction.

From the very beginning, the expedition to Ostankino was an act of adventurism. Several days earlier, during one of the meetings in the White House, someone had pointed out that nothing in the country was being guarded as rigorously as the television center. This was the regime's center of power, its holiest of holys. On orders from the government, an armed unit made for Ostankino along the same streets by which the demonstrators were heading for the television center. Thousands of people cheered the military trucks as they passed, thinking the troops had crossed over to the side of the parliament. No one on the government side attempted to block the road to the television center, or to hold up the protesters.

The main forces which the authorities had brought in to defend the center were not stationed in the building, but some distance from it. It is not hard to see why this was done; the supporters of the parliament would be drawn into clashes, and then after firing had broken out, the main government forces would be brought into action. This was precisely what happened. The demonstrators were allowed to burst into the television center. Six armored personnel carriers stood quietly by, not yet having received the order to open fire on the crowd. The APCs were joined by a further fifteen armored vehicles. Then several hundred troops from the Vityaz special forces detachment raked the crowd with gunfire. The slaughter continued for several hours. The Yeltsin forces lost three people. On the square in front of the television center dozens of people were killed, most of them unarmed.

Inside the television center, the studios of Radio Resonance were destroyed by fire. This was Moscow's only independent radio station; not long before, the authorities had shut it down because it had carried broadcasts by Rutskoy and other opposition figures. At the time of the October events, Radio Resonance had just been allowed back on air.

By midnight the shooting at Ostankino had come to an end. Units faithful to Yeltsin were being assembled for the assault on the White House.

24

THAT SUNDAY morning I was not in Moscow. I had gone for the day to visit my family outside the city, and I only managed to return towards eight in the evening. By that time shooting had already broken out around Ostankino, two of the news channels were off the air, and one was broadcasting a flower pattern. When I went to the building of the Krasnopresnenskiy Regional Council, there was hardly anyone there. The OMON had gone over to the side of the parliament, and had been sent off somewhere else. With the breaking of the blockade, the deputies of the Russian Federation had flocked into the White House.

On the office door of the chairperson of the regional council, Aleksandr Krasnov, was a decree of President Rutskoy under which Krasnov was named mayor of Moscow. This had been Krasnov's cherished dream. When Popov resigned in 1992, Krasnov had put forward his candidacy for mayor and even conducted an election campaign, although it was clear to everyone that there wouldn't be any elections. Expensive, colorful posters with Krasnov's portrait, "the candidate of the Party of Muscovites," were pasted up around the city. Some incalculable sum was spent, but to no result—Yeltsin simply appointed Luzhkov to take Popov's place. Now, without having been elected, Krasnov could feel that he was the ruler of the city—at least for a few hours.

After congratulating Krasnov on his appointment, I asked him which particular city services were under his control. It became clear that even the new administrator of the Russian capital had no idea. "You try and work it out," he urged. Sadly, there was nothing left to do but follow his advice. By this time, Vladimir Kondratov had arrived, along with Aleksandr Segal, the Press Secretary of the Federation of Independent Trade Unions of Russia. We set off together to the White House, hoping that there, at least, we could obtain some information.

A multitude of unarmed people were swarming around the parliament building discussing the latest news. Then, unexpectedly, commandeered trucks appeared, full of agitated people demanding weapons. They reported that there had been dozens of dead and wounded at Ostankino, and they were asking for help. Receiving neither weapons nor assistance, they once again set off for somewhere else. Within the White House itself, chaos reigned. As before, there were no lights. During the afternoon, after the lifting of the blockade, the lights had been turned on temporarily. The elevators were not working, so we climbed the stairs.

In a corridor on one of the upper floors, we came upon General Albert Makashov, whom the pro-Yeltsin press later named as one of the main instigators of the "carefully planned and prepared revolt." The general was running down the corridor, fastening up a bulletproof vest as he went, shouting: "I don't have any weapons! I don't have any people! There won't be any help! Go and install soviet power yourselves!"

In the Kremlin that same evening, Sergey Parkhomenko, a journalist for the newspaper *Segodnya*, witnessed a similar spectacle. Among government leaders, panic reigned; Yeltsin, apparently, had completely lost control of the situation and was merely questioning those around him in order to find out what was going on. Parkhomenko said it was like a madhouse.

Some time later, however, the "gray cardinals" of the regime, Gennadiy Burbulis and Mikhail Poltoranin, appeared in the Kremlin. They assumed command and quickly enforced order among the distracted members of the government. These two knew perfectly well that there was no serious threat. Rutskoy did not have any serious forces, and the people who had obeyed his summons and gone to Ostankino had fallen into a trap. Burbulis and Poltoranin had triumphed. All that now remained for them to do was to put down the revolt and to settle accounts with their adversaries, teaching a lesson to anyone who might dare to speak out against the regime for a long time to come.

While we were still in the Krasnopresnenskiy Regional Council, we had learned that Luzhkov's forces were blockading the Mossoviet. The members of the anti-crisis staff had been locked in their offices. Meanwhile, Vice Premier Yegor Gaidar had used the second television channel, the only one that was working, to summon supporters of the regime to gather outside the Mossoviet. These "volunteers" were to help the OMON capture the building. They behaved in an extremely aggressive, even boorish manner.

Meanwhile, after failing to obtain coherent information about what was happening in the city, Segal, Kondratov, and I found a ride in a car that was going to the Oktyabrskaya Regional Council. There we met with Dmitriy Krymov and other regional deputies, whom we knew well because of their opposition to corrupt property deals around Gagarin Square. The conversations we had in the regional council building did not increase our optimism. Troops were being brought in to the center of the city, while the supporters of the parliament were mostly unarmed and without real leadership.

While we were sitting with our colleagues from the regional council, armored personnel carriers were passing along Leninskiy Prospekt. The chairperson of the regional council tried to discover whether the machines bore the insignia of guard units. If there were, this meant the vehicles belonged to the Tamanskaya division. If not, that meant they belonged to the interior ministry forces. As if that now had the slightest significance.

Leaving the building of the regional council, we stopped next to the vehicle that had brought us from the White House. This was a four-wheel-drive UAZ belonging to the militia. Supporters of both the parliament and Yeltsin had many of these vehicles, since both the White House guard and Luzhkov's OMON were considered subunits of the militia. A number of other activists who had also come from the White House were standing with us near the vehicle. Some of them proposed that we return to the parliament, others suggested that we visit other regional councils, and still others thought we should disperse and head home.

While we were holding this discussion, a car stopped next to us. Four people in civilian clothing, carrying automatic rifles, leapt out. They wore bulletproof vests over their jackets. Two of them smelled strongly of liquor. Next, a man in the uniform of a militia colonel (minus the cap), with a large old-style automatic rifle, climbed out. Astonishingly enough, he really was a militia officer. After cocking his rifle, he ordered us to put our hands up and stand in line.

Threatening to "blow our brains out" if we so much as moved, the guardians of law and order searched us, and then, in two vehicles which had driven up, took us to Militia Station No. 2 in the Polyanka neighborhood. Here they stood us with our faces to the wall, and after hitting us around the legs and on our backs a few times as a warning, led us off to be interrogated separately. They questioned us on how we came to be next to a militia vehicle, on where we had been before we came to the regional council, and on our political views.

Our deputies' cards did not arouse any respect from them—rather the reverse. While one militia member was questioning me in proper fashion, another ran into the room from time to time and slammed his fist into my back or head. Then he again ran off somewhere about his business, but on the way back burst in on us again and hit me once more. This was accompanied by shouts such as, "You wanted democracy, you sons of bitches? We'll show you democracy!" Among themselves, the militia members used criminals' slang, and did not refer to one another except as "dicks" and "pigs." In the militia station the next day, we met a racketeer who had been arrested. This man, by contrast, spoke proper Russian.

After questioning and beating us some more, the guardians of law and order from Militia Station No. 2 admitted that they had nothing on us. But they could not let us go since a curfew was in force and it was already midnight. They promised to release us in the morning. They took our valuables, notebooks, and deputies' cards, saying that they would return them in the morning. We were led off to the cells.

The next morning, instead of setting us free as promised, they loaded us into a militia UAZ with our hands bound behind our backs, and took us off to Militia Station No. 77. Here they informed me that under a Yeltsin decree the Moscow City Council had been disbanded, the immunity of deputies had been revoked, and we were charged with stealing a militia vehicle. The UAZ in which we had travelled from the White House had, it turned out, been abandoned by the militia near Ostankino. It had then been used to transport wounded, and had made several trips to one place and another with constantly changing drivers.

Leonid Ilyushenko, the last behind the wheel, had been given the vehicle at the White House by one of the commanders of the spontaneously formed volunteer corps. He could not say precisely where the vehicle had come from either, but after he had been interrogated under torture, the militia explained everything to him. Almost unconscious from the blows, he signed a number of statements to the effect that he had stolen the vehicle at the instigation of Moscow City Council deputies Kondratov and Kagarlitsky. These maleficent deputies, showing him their identity cards, had forced him to hijack the militia UAZ. Along with gun-toting companions, they had then driven about the city issuing orders to armed insurgents.

At the same time as the investigators' evidence accused us of driving around the capital, more than a dozen people had seen us in totally different places. I had mostly been at the dacha, while Kondratov was working in the Krasnopresnenskiy Regional Soviet many kilometers from Ostankino. The affair was not about us at all. Compromising evidence was needed against the Moscow City Council, in order to explain to the public why it had been necessary to disband the Council and deprive the deputies of their immunity. All that remained was to obtain open confessions from us.

Kondratov and Segal were handcuffed and beaten with clubs on the back and legs. Then Kondratov had his head beaten against a bulletproof vest. I was not spared—they hit my head against a grating and against a wall, and then beat me on the shoulders with a rifle butt. After the second blow I almost fell to the floor. This could have ended very badly, had not one of the militia members literally torn me from the hands of his colleagues. Another militia member in an army bulletproof vest dragged me from the room where the beatings were going on and pushed me into a cell with the others.

However severely they beat the deputies, they beat the other prisoners more ferociously. This was to milk them for new statements against us, and to serve as a warning. All the people who had been passengers in the UAZ were being held in one place. Other people who had been arrested in different places were also dragged in here, in some cases totally at random. Unwilling to investigate each separate case, they listed all the detainees as "passengers in a militia vehicle." Soon the number of "passengers" on the list reached fourteen. That UAZ seemed destined for a place in the Guinness Book of World Records.

We sat behind the bars. Shouts and the sound of blows, accompanied by swearing, carried from the corridor. This alternated with reports on the militia radio, which spoke of the storming of the White House and hundreds dead in the city. One of the militia officers brought two grenades into the militia station, and every militia officer who came in tried without fail to discover how these were supposed to work. The militia called in the army engineers, but the engineers were delayed; meanwhile, the weary and occasionally half-drunk minions of the law several times came close to blowing up themselves and us together.

As long as no one knew where we were being held, the militia could do whatever they wanted with us. Toward evening, the racketeer who spoke proper Russian was able to help us out. He managed to smuggled out our home phone numbers which we had written on his hand, and which, upon his release, he called. My wife then contacted several friends and the leadership of the trade unions. Within a few minutes all the details of our fate were in the international computer networks. After another half-hour, telephone calls started pouring into the militia station from Tokyo, London, and New York, from foreign newspapers and human rights organizations. Some time later, a phone call came from the presidential administration demanding that the scandal be quelled immediately. Presidential Council member Sergey Karaganov, arriving in a luxurious BMW, explained to the militia chief that it was imperative for the deputies to be released. This independent initiative later cost Karaganov serious unpleasantness; he had not been appointed to the Presidential Council in order to defend the rights of oppositionists.

Soon, the militia member on duty took to answering the incessant calls by repeating distractedly, "They've already been released." "It's not true!" we shouted from behind the bars. Eventually, we were freed along with all the prisoners except the driver of the UAZ, out of whom the militia now began beating new affidavits.

Late on the night of October 4 we made it home. By this time the White House had already fallen, and a new order reigned in the city. The Mossoviet had been seized late in the evening of October 3, roughly an hour after we had been arrested. The guards submitted to the orders from the mayor and behaved in proper fashion. The "volunteers," on the other hand, showed themselves in their true colors. Several offices were sacked and looted. One of the guards who tried to stop the excesses of the democratic activists was beaten up.

All the members of the anti-crisis team were arrested after remaining at their posts until the last minute. Among those arrested was the human rights defender Viktor Bulgakov, who was first imprisoned in 1952, while Stalin was still alive. Others detained included Lena Klimenko and Yury Khramov, who had been promised awards for their previous defense of the White House; the former dissident Viktor Kuzin; and the former KGB officer Aleksandr Tsopov. Deputy Chairperson of the Moscow City Council Yury Sedykh-Bondarenko was one of the last to leave the building. First he was blockaded in his office; then he was removed and, after interrogation, sent to prison. Aleksandr Popov was luckier. The guards got him out of the cordoned-off building. He issued the last report of the Press Center of the Moscow City Council from a pay telephone on the street.

The premises and equipment of the press center were promptly handed over to the press service of the mayor's office. Here, a real pogrom was staged. Not only were papers pulled from the shelves and everything turned upside down, but for some reason a fax machine had been burned out.

The pro-Yeltsin newspaper *Segodnya* admitted that rebels who were under fire at Ostankino were leaving the scene of the shooting, going up to commercial kiosks in a totally peaceful fashion, buying chocolate and Coca-Cola, and then going back under fire. Everything changed when the city was under the control of the defenders of order and property. Robberies began occurring. The actions of an OMON unit from the city of Lipetsk were particularly outrageous: militia members broke into stores and money-changing offices, and terrorized street traders. Mafia leaders complained about the lawlessness that reigned in the capital. One of the crime lords later recounted that during those October days he had received a plea over the telephone. "The militia are making a raid, they're smashing the place up and stealing everything," cried a terrified stall operator. "You've got to restore order! Send a gang immediately!"

25

THE STORMING of the White House began on the morning of October 4, when armored personnel carriers of the Russian Army opened fire on the crowd that had gathered next to the parliament building. Then tanks drove up. The crews were made up of volunteer officers—the authorities did not trust enlisted men or NCOs.

The shooting continued for several hours. The attackers were firing from cannon and from heavy-caliber machine guns. While hundreds of unarmed people were hiding from the gunfire in the parliament basement, more and more new forces were brought onto the scene. A fire broke out on the upper floors. A library, an archive, and a computer center went up in flames. How many people died there remains unknown.

Despite the intense shooting, several thousand people tried to break through to the White House. They were driven back by machine-gun fire. Behind the government forces, meanwhile, crowds of onlookers gathered, marveling at the spectacle of the burning parliament. And because food stores close to the scene of the shooting had cut their prices dramatically, many people risked their lives crawling under the bullets to obtain butter or sausage for half price.

Later, when censorship was lifted, *Nezavisimaya Gazeta*—which, in another Russian paradox, had moved sharply to the left and grown much bolder despite threats and pressures—published a series of eyewitness accounts, including some from soldiers who had taken part in the attack. An officer of the Interior Ministry forces spoke of hundreds of corpses being taken secretly from the White House and burned outside the city. Another officer, a colonel working in the Russian Defence Ministry, described how he and his colleagues hid in their offices, closing the windows and trying not to hear the crash of exploding shells and the noise of patrolling helicopters.

The authorities declared that in the course of two days, 142 people were killed in Moscow. This was a mockery—the real number of dead had to have been several times greater. No one even tried to determine the precise number who were wounded and beaten. Thousands were arrested. During the assault, soldiers looted and smashed up all the stores around the White House; these stores had not been touched during two weeks of demonstrations. Residential buildings were raked constantly with fire from government forces. In some apartments, dozens of bullets were later removed from the walls—the building at 5 Devyatinsky Lane suffered particular damage. In some apartments, whole handfuls of bullets were collected; eyewitnesses reported that these were of the dirtiest variety. They had hollow centers which made them more dangerous than their legalized counterparts. Residents took to their stairwells to escape the gunfire. One building caught fire, but the troops did not allow the firefighters through until half the building had burned.

By 5:30 p.m., on October 4, the leaders of the parliament had surrendered. Together with them, the deputies and pro-parliament activists were brought out of the building. Most of those who were arrested were beaten. Parliamentary speaker Ruslan Khasbulatov, Aleksandr Rutskoy, and a few other people were taken off to Lefortovo Prison. There they were placed under the care of the Russian Security Ministry, the former KGB. This ministry was headed by Sergey Balashov, the same Balashov who ten years earlier, in this very Lefortovo Prison, had interrogated me on charges of anti-Soviet activity. Now he was entrusted with rooting out the "Communist infection."

In Moscow, the authorities declared a state of emergency,

imposing a curfew and censorship. The newspapers *Nezavisimaya Gazeta*, *Segodnya*, and *Komsomolskaya Pravda* came out with blank spaces. These papers, however, were relatively lucky; all the opposition dailies were shut down completely. This was the case not only with the Communist *Pravda*, *Sovetskaya Rossiya*, and *Glasnost*, but also with the very moderate *Rabochaya Tribuna*. Communist organizations and the centrist People's Party of Free Russia were banned. From this time on, all political parties were forced to apply to the Russian Ministry of Justice to obtain a certificate stating that they had not been outlawed. The Constitutional Court was suspended. Not only the Moscow City Council and the regional councils were dissolved, but also the self-management committees that had dealt with minor everyday matters.

From that point on, television and radio did not provide airtime to anyone but representatives of the authorities. People who were anxious to find out what was really happening once again could only tune in to Radio Liberty from Munich during its evening broadcast hours.

The state of emergency was accompanied by the expulsion of hundreds of foreigners from the capital. People from the Caucasus who were accused of violating the internal passport system were beaten and thrown out of the city. Under Russian laws the passport requirements had long since been abolished, but this did not deter anyone. The OMON warriors sauntered openly about the Moscow markets, taking from the stalls of foreign traders any goods that caught their fancy. Hundreds of people saw what was happening, but did not dare protest. All this was called "the struggle against the Caucasian mafia." Meanwhile, our own Moscow mafia went calmly about its business.

On television and in the newspapers, distinguished intellectuals one after another declared their complete support for the regime. The only point on which they criticized the government was for its excessive liberalism and softness with regard to the vanquished.

The unanimity of the Russian intelligentsia was matched

only by the universal approval with which Western leaders greeted Yeltsin's coup. None of these leaders expressed any sympathy for the thousands of peaceful citizens who suffered during the coup. The leaders of the "free world" did not see anything wrong in the Russian parliament being shelled by tanks, nor in the violation of the constitution, nor in the acts of lawlessness being committed in Moscow.

Whatever might have been the errors and misdeeds of the Russian parliament, nothing can justify the stance taken by the Western politicians who applauded the liquidation of democracy in Russia. If Russia has suffered a political and economic catastrophe, the moral catastrophe of the West is no less great. Western leaders publicly and solemnly repudiated the principles of constitutional rule, of the law-governed state, and of the freedoms and rights of the individual.

The West does not seem to care about the prospects of true democracy in the East. It seems consistently to do everything in order to turn us, as Moscow Soviet deputy Aleksandr Kalinin put it, into "a banana republic in which you can't grow bananas."

The opposition, with Rutskoy and Khasbulatov at its head, met with defeat. It deserved this debacle. Even if Burbulis and other scriptwriters of the October events consciously provoked the clashes of October 3, even if they deliberately created in the supporters of the parliament the illusion that they had won, and pushed them into reckless actions, who forced the leaders of the parliamentary camp to submit to this provocation?

Nor is the question simply one of the incompetence and irresponsibility of the parliamentary leaders. Had these political forces not supported Yeltsin? Had they not approved the senseless policy of universal privatization? And had they not adopted, one after the other, laws which gave the mayor of Moscow and the president of Russia virtually unlimited power?

The Moscow City Council was doomed to perish along with the Supreme Soviet. Although the Moscow deputies began to perceive the dangers earlier than their parliamentary colleagues, the same fate awaited them.

But on the morning of October 5, as I went down into the

metro, I was allowed as usual to pass through the barrier without paying after I had shown my deputy's accreditation. Underground, the constitution was still in force. The government could bombard the parliament and disband the council, but it could not manage to abolish free travel for deputies on the public transportation system.

"Nothing's going to work for them!" I thought.

Post Scriptum

Moscow has survived a lot. It was destroyed and burned down many times, but even after it burned to the ground in 1812, contemporaries of the fire were able to say ironically that the fire "aided its beautification considerably." The city survived Stalin's "reconstruction," in the course of which hundreds of historical buildings were destroyed, magnificent churches and monasteries blown up. Moscow remained itself—an eclectic, turbulent, and, despite everything, beautiful city.

Under its first mayor, Moscow, never known for its cleanliness and order, became a phantasmagorical city where its rats and cockroaches felt more comfortable than its people. It was impossible to walk two hundred meters in the center of town without seeing abandoned buildings with knocked-out windows. Fires became a constant threat like in the old days, and crime rose to a level similar to that of Chicago during the Prohibition.

The rule of Popov and the Russian Democrats turned the capital's streets into a giant flea market, where one could literally not make a step without bumping into yet another trader. There were fewer and fewer goods and more and more people selling them. Scared by the growing disorder, the mayor's office attempted to halt the "free trade" in the streets. The traders disappeared for a while, taking their goods with them.

If under Luzhkov there was a bit more order, this was accomplished only through arbitrary measures on the part of the administration and the police. Even the entrepreneurs, having had a taste of the wonders of the Russian market, were starting to complain that they could not work normally under such conditions.

In the new Moscow, millionaires live as safely and comfortably as in any other impoverished city of the capitalist world. They prefer to put off thinking about the fact that sooner or later the starved average citizen will present a bill that even the holders of fantastic fortunes will be unable to pay. But they are gradually acquiring apartments in New York and in other places that seem safer to them. Sooner or later, their rule will come to an end. This is as inevitable as was the collapse of the Communist regime.

It was in Moscow that the collapse of Communist rule began; it was in Moscow that the ascent of the new oligarchy, which called itself "democratic," began—and it is Moscow where, its descent—or, at least, its crisis—is beginning. The most difficult and possibly the most frightening part is still ahead of us. But there is hope. And that means that we must fight on.